David Goodman is Professor of Asian Studies at Murdoch University, Western Australia. Educated at the universities of Manchester, Beijing and London he has written and edited a number of books on Chinese politics and society. He is a member of the editorial boards of *The China Quarterly*, the *Journal of Communist Studies* and the *Pacific Review* and is currently working on the politics of the Taihang Revolutionary Base Area.

Other titles in the series *Makers of the Twentieth Century* in Cardinal:

Brandt Barbara Marshall
de Gaulle Julian Jackson
Martin Luther King Adam Fairclough
Nkrumah David Birmingham
Roosevelt Fiona Venn

Forthcoming titles in the same series:

Trotsky David Law
Khrushchev Martin McCauley
Tito Stevan K. Pavlowitch
Nehru Denis Judd
Jinnah Howard Brasted
Atatürk Alan Palmer
Smuts Iain Smith
Lenin Beryl Williams
Adenauer Andrew Crozier

Makers of the Twentieth Century

Deng Xiaoping

DAVID GOODMAN

CaRDÍNaL

To Sushu

A CARDINAL Book

First published in Great Britain in Cardinal by Sphere Books Ltd 1990

Copyright © David S.G. Goodman 1990

Although every effort has been made to contact
copyright holders of all material used in this book,
the publishers would be pleased to hear from any
copyright holders whom we have been unable to trace
if their material appears in this book.

All rights reserved.
No part of this publication may be reproduced,
stored in a retrieval system, or transmitted, in any
form or by any means without the prior
permission in writing of the publisher, nor be
otherwise circulated in any form of binding or
cover other than that in which it is published and
without a similar condition including this
condition being imposed on the subsequent
purchaser.

Typeset by Leaper & Gard Ltd, Bristol
Printed and bound in Great Britain by
Cox & Wyman Ltd, Reading

ISBN 0 7474 0400 3

Sphere Books Ltd
A Division of
Macdonald & Co (Publishers) Ltd
Orbit House
1 New Fetter Lane
London EC4A 1AR
A member of Maxwell Macmillan Pergamon Publishing Corporation

Contents

	Editor's Foreword	vi
	Chronology	viii
	Map of China	xii
	Abbreviations	xiv
	Preface	xv
	Introduction: Deng Xiaoping, Communism and Revolution	1
1	Formative political years, 1920–49	30
2	General Secretary of the CCP, 1949–60	56
3	On the 'Capitalist Road', 1960–6	76
4	The pendulum years, 1969–78	93
5	Reform and reaction, 1979–89	111
6	Comrade Deng: a preliminary assessment	135
	References	152
	Select Bibliography	161
	Index	164

Editor's Foreword

The last decade of the century is a good moment to look back at some of the dominating individuals who have shaped the modern world. *Makers of the Twentieth Century* is a series of short biographical reassessments, written by specialists but aimed at a wide general audience. We hope that they will be useful to sixth-formers and students seeking a brief introduction to a new subject; but also to the ordinary reader looking for the minimum she or he needs to know of the life and legacy of the century's key figures, in a form that can be absorbed in a single sitting. At the same time we hope that the interpretations, based on the latest research – even where there is not space to display it – will be of sufficient interest to command the attention of other specialists.

The series will eventually cover all the outstanding heroes and villains of the century. They can, as a sort of party game, be sorted into three – or perhaps four – types. Some can be classed primarily as national leaders, who either restored the failing destinies of old nations (de Gaulle, Adenauer, Kemal Atatürk) or created new ones out of the collapse of the European empires (Nkrumah, Jinnah). Others were national leaders first of all, but made a still greater impact on the international stage (Franklin Roosevelt, Willy Brandt, Jan Smuts). A further category were not heads of government at all, but achieved worldwide resonance as the embodiments of powerful ideas (Trotsky, Martin Luther King). The great tyrants, however, (Hitler, Stalin, Mao Zedong) are not easily contained in any category but transcend them all.

The series, too, aims to leap categories, attempting to place each subject in a double focus, both in relation to the domestic politics of his or her own country and as an actor on the world stage – whether as builder or destroyer, role model or prophet. One consequence of the communications revolution in this century has been that the charismatic leaders of quite small countries (Castro, Ho Chi Minh, Gadaffi) can command a following well beyond the frontiers of their national constituency.

At the centre of each volume stands the individual: of course biography can be a distorting mirror, exaggerating the influence of human agency on vast impersonal events; yet unquestionably there are, as Shakespeare's Brutus observed, tides in the affairs of men 'which, taken at the flood, lead on to fortune'. At critical moments the course of history can be diverted, channelled or simply ridden by individuals who by luck, ruthlessness or destiny are able to impose their personality, for good or ill, upon their times. Who can doubt that Lenin and Hitler, Mao and Gorbachev – to name but four – have decisively, at least for a time, bent the history of our epoch to their will? These, with men and women from every major country in the world, are the *Makers of the Twentieth Century*.

John Campbell
London, 1990

Chronology

1904 Deng Xixian born in Guang'an County, Sichuan Province, China
1920 Leaves China for France on a work-study programme
1922 Joins Socialist Young League of China
1924 Joins Chinese Communist Party
1926 Leaves France for Moscow
1927 Returns to China and Xian Military & Political Academy
      Becomes secretary of the CCP Central Committee in Hankou
      Changes name to Deng Xiaoping
      Moves with CCP Central Committee to Shanghai
      Chief secretary of CCP Central Committee
      Marries Zhang Xianyuan
1929 Goes to Guangxi as CCP organizer, as Deng Bin Zhang Xianyuan dies
      Organizes Bose Uprising, the Right River Soviet and the 7th Red Army in Guangxi
1930 Organizes Longzhou Uprising, the Left River Soviet and the 8th Red Army in Guangxi
      Leads merged 7th Red Army troops toward Jiangxi
1931 Goes to Shanghai to report to CCP Central Committee
      Secretary, CCP Committee, Ruijin County
1932 Marries Jin Weiying
      Secretary, CCP Committee Huichang County

Deng Xiaoping

	Director, Propaganda Department, CCP Committee Jiangxi Province
1933	Disciplined as follower of Luo Ming and sent to work in the Nancun District Party Committee, Le'an County
	Jin Weiying divorces Deng
1934	Secretary-General, General Political Department, 1st Front Army
	Assigned to work in Propaganda Division, General Political Department, Red Army
	Editor-in-chief, *Red Star*
	Appointed Chief Secretary, CCP Central Committee
1935	Chief, Propaganda Division, Political Department, First Army Group, Red Army
1936	Deputy Director, Political Department, First Army Group
	Director, Political Department, First Army Group
1937	Deputy Director, Political Department, 8th Route Army
	Political Commissar 129th Division, 8th Route Army
1938	Attends Enlarged 6th Plenum of 6th Central Committee of CCP in Yan'an
1939	Attends Enlarged Meeting of CCP Political Bureau in Yan'an
	Marries Zhuo Lin in Yan'an
1942	Secretary, Taihang Sub-Bureau of the CCP Central Committee
1943	Acting Secretary, North China Bureau, CCP Central Committee
1945	Secretary, Shanxi–Hebei–Shandong–Henan Bureau of the CCP Central Committee
	Political Commissar, Shanxi–Hebei–Shandong–Henan Military Command
	Elected to 7th Central Committee, CCP, at 7th CCP Congress in Yan'an

Chronology

1947   Shanxi–Hebei–Shandong–Henan Field Army crosses Yellow River and marches south to Dabie Mountains

1948   Secretary, Frontline Committee, Huai-Hai Campaign

1949   1st Secretary, East China Bureau CCP Central Committee

1st Secretary, South-west Bureau CCP Central Committee Member, Central People's Government Council; and Revolutionary Military Council

1950   Vice Chairman, Southwest Military & Administrative Committee

Political Commissar, Southwest Military Command

1952   Vice-Premier (to 1966)

Vice-Chairman, Finance and Economic Commission

1952   Member, State Planning Commission (to 1954)

1953   Minister of Finance (to 1954)

Director of the Office of Communications

1954   Secretary General, CCP Central Committee Vice-Chairman, National Defence Council (to 1966)

Director, Organization Department, CCP

1955   Member, CCP Political Bureau

1956   Visits Moscow for 20th CPSU Congress

8th CCP Congress: General Secretary of CCP; member, Standing Committee, CCP Political Bureau

1957   Visits Moscow for Celebrations to mark 40th Anniversary of October Revolution and Moscow Summit

1960   Deputy Head (under Liu Shaoqi) of delegation to Moscow Conference of Communist Parties

1961   Head of delegation to North Korea

1963   Head of delegation to Moscow (with Peng Zhen and Kang Sheng)

Deng Xiaoping

1963	Acting Premier, State Council (to 1964)
1965	Head of delegation to Romania
1966	Removed from leadership of CCP
1969	Sent to do manual labour in Xinjian County, Jiangxi Province
1973	Appointed Vice-Premier, State Council
	Elected to 10th Central Committee
1974	Elected to 10th CCP Political Bureau
	Head, delegation to UN Special Session on Problems of Materials and Development
1975	Member, Standing Committee, CCP Political Bureau; and Vice-Chairman, CCP Central Committee
	1st Vice Premier
	Chief-of-staff, PLA
	Head of delegation to France
1976	Removed from leadership after Tiananmen Incident
1977	Re-instated as Vice-Chairman, CCP Central Committee; Vice-Premier, State Council; Vice-Chairman, Military Commission; Chief-of-Staff, PLA
1978	Head of delegation to Burma and Nepal
	Head of delegation to North Korea
	Head of delegation to Japan
	Head of delegation to Thailand, Malaysia and Singapore
1978	Chairman, Chinese People's Political Consultative Conference (to 1983)
1979	Head of delegation to USA and Japan
1980	Steps down as Chief of Staff, PLA; Vice-Premier
1981	Chairman, CCP Military Affairs Committee (to 1989)
1982	Member, Standing Committee, 12th CCP Political Bureau
1982	Chairman, CCP Advisory Committee (to 1987)
1983	Chairman, Central Military Commission (to 1989)
1989	Retires from all public offices

Map of China

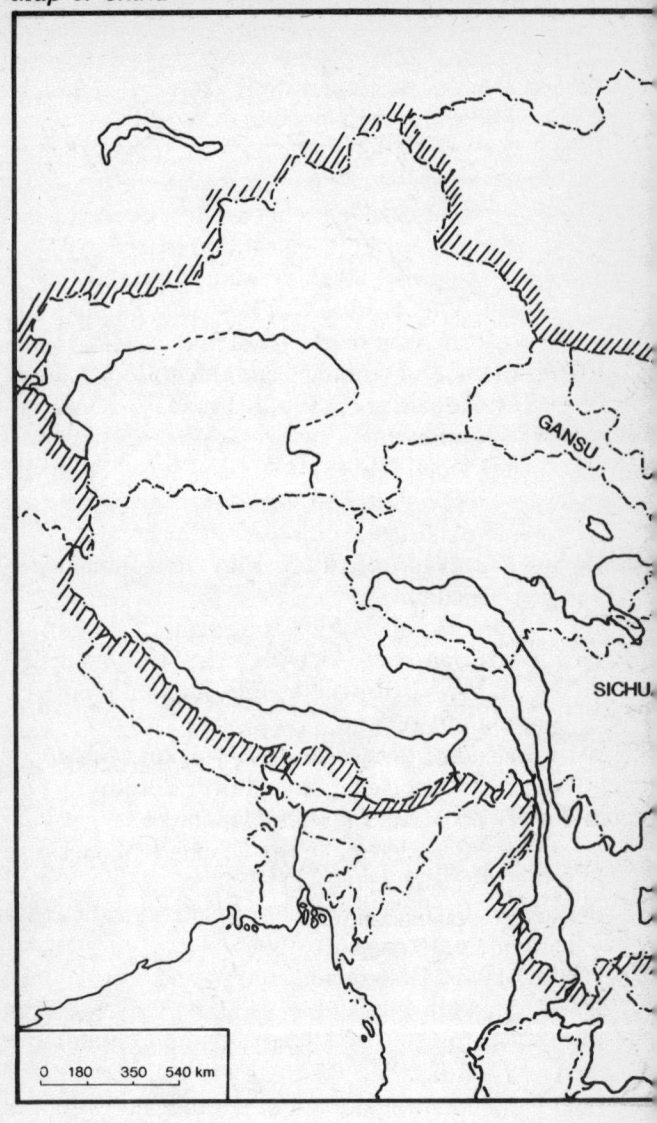

Abbreviations

CCP   Chinese Communist Party
CPSU   Communist Party of the Soviet Union
PLA   People's Liberation Army
PRC   People's Republic of China

Preface

The legend of Yan'an – the Chinese Communist Party's [CCP] capital during the Sino-Japanese War of 1937–45 – is one of the most enduring of Chinese politics. Yan'an was where Mao Zedong consolidated his leadership of the CCP, and the base from which the CCP finally came to rule China. The policies and practices used to mobilize the population, wage war on the Japanese and win support for the CCP rapidly achieved legendary status, as did those who had led the party. An essential part of the legend is that these were formative years for the CCP and its leaders. The shared experiences – the difficulties which the CCP faced as well as the ways in which it overcame them – created not simply a united leadership but a strong feeling of solidarity.

It is a legend which the CCP has never been slow to capitalize on. Since 1949 the CCP has constantly referred to its Yan'an heritage to emphasize not only its own traditions but also its close relationship with the rest of the population. Even during the Cultural Revolution the CCP stressed the stability of politics based on its Yan'an leadership. One result outside China is that the Yan'an experience has often been regarded as the base-line for description of Chinese politics well into the 1980s.

Deng Xiaoping is usually considered a political supporter of Mao Zedong, and hence part of that Yan'an leadership. He certainly shared in the experiences of the Sino-Japanese War, but not for the most part in Yan'an. Deng was in the Shanxi-Hebei-Shandong-Henan Border Region, centred on the Taihang Revolutionary Base Area, for almost all the Sino-Japanese War and spent less than a year in Yan'an during 1937. Thereafter he only visited on four brief occasions and was not even recalled for the major party rectification campaign of 1942-3.

In an important sense, and despite the rhetoric of Chinese politics, it was not necessary to have been in Yan'an to be considered part of the Yan'an leadership, or even the Yan'an tradition. Most of the leaders of the CCP in the field spent much of their time outside Yan'an, though admittedly all but Deng appear to have gone there to participate in the rectification campaign which sinicized the CCP and consolidated Mao's leadership. Moreover, Yan'an was a legend which the CCP deliberately set out to create. The Shaanxi-Gansu-Ningxia Border Region, based on Yan'an, was designed from the start as a model for the other border regions and base areas established during the Sino-Japanese War to emulate. Its unique features, particularly its small size, its homogeneity and security from Japanese invasion, made it a suitable testing ground for the rest of the CCP.

Nonetheless, an important theme in this biography of Deng Xiaoping is that his career after 1949 owed more to his Taihang experience than to being part of the Yan'an tradition of the CCP. It is not that Deng did not have good relations with the CCP leaders, such as Mao, who were based in Yan'an. On the contrary, his relations were clearly for the most part very good indeed. However, after 1949 and more particularly during and after the Cultural Revolution, the associations Deng had made in the Taihang Base Area and its border region became

Preface

more important. Moreover, though the policies Deng implemented in Taihang and its border region during the Sino–Japanese War often drew their inspiration from Yan'an, the different conditions and problems he encountered provided Deng with a somewhat different set of perspectives on the politics of change. In the debates of post-revolutionary China those differences were to become important determinants of Deng's political stance and his fate.

As the text details, Deng has gone by several names during his life, and Deng Xiaoping was not the one originally chosen for him by his family. Nonetheless, to avoid confusion he has been consistently referred to by that name throughout. Similarly, though of considerably less significance, the CCP's English translation of the term for its leading institution changed during the 1980s from 'politburo' to 'political bureau'. Again to avoid confusion, the latter term has been used consistently.

In the Sino–Japanese War, border regions, border areas and base areas were established by the CCP behind enemy lines. On the whole border regions were larger than both border areas and base areas and in the case of the Shanxi–Hebei–Shandong–Henan Border Region contained several border areas and base areas. However, the system of nomenclature is inherently confusing. The terms for 'region' and 'area' in Chinese are often translated into English interchangeably. Moreover, the conditions of guerilla warfare often meant that border regions, border areas and even base areas (which were supposed to be more stable) fluctuated wildly in size. To complicate matters even further, border regions and areas were so designated for two reasons: they bordered the enemy, initially the Japanese and after 1945 the Nationalist Party; and they were established on the borders of various provinces. Thus, the Shanxi–Hebei–Shandong–Henan Border Region was located where those provinces meet.

Deng Xiaoping

During the Sino-Japanese War and for some time after Deng was the ranking political cadre of the Shanxi-Hebei-Shandong-Henan Border Region which had been established on and included the Taihang Revolutionary Base Area. Not least because the border region had such a long name both will be referred to as Taihang, though maintaining the distinction between border region and base area. Taihang is thus used to describe the Shanxi-Hebei-Shandong-Henan Border Region in the same way that Yan'an refers to the Shaanxi-Gansu-Ningxia Border Region.

Three further explanations may help readers unfamiliar with the politics of the CCP. The term 'cadre' in this context refers to an official of party or state. CCP Central Committees and their meetings are numbered after the CCP Congress which elected them. Thus the 3rd Plenum of the 11th Central Committee, refers to the third full and formal meeting of the central committee elected by the 11th CCP Congress of 1977. In the term Mao Zedong Thought, the 'Thought' refers to ideology (or rather a specific kind of ideology) in Chinese. Mao Zedong Thought is thus to be differentiated from Mao Zedong's thoughts, his personal ideas or actions.

In general the *pinyin* system of romanization has been used for Chinese throughout this book. The exceptions are names more familiarly rendered otherwise – notably Canton and Chiang Kai-shek – and references to publications and quotations which have employed other methods of transliteration, where the original has been cited.

At the request of the general editor of the series in which this book appears, references and footnotes have been kept to a minimum. To assist the reader unfamiliar with Chinese but interested in pursuing some of the sources, wherever possible, reference has been provided to English language translations of Chinese sources.

Acknowledgement is due to Rod MacFarquhar and

Preface

John Campbell who first pointed me in the direction of this project, and colleagues in Taiyuan who introduced me to the history of the Taihang Revolutionary Base Area. Research into Deng's life, and the writing of this book have all taken place since I arrived at Murdoch University in July 1988, and I would like to acknowledge the university's help and support particularly in allowing leave to carry out research in Hong Kong.

My thanks must also go to several colleagues, who though they bear no responsibility for the final product, have given willingly of their advice and encouragement: Bev Hooper and Tim Wright of Murdoch University; Gerry Segal of Bristol University and Chatham House, London; Marisa Bantjes of the University of Newcastle-upon-Tyne; James Cotton and You Ji of the Australian National University. Last but by no means least, my greatest debt is to my wife, Susan, who only very occasionally objects to a house peopled by the ghosts of the 8th Route Army.

David Goodman
Murdoch University, Western Australia
February 1990

Introduction: Deng Xiaoping, Communism and Revolution

Deng Xiaoping has been the effective leader of both the Chinese Communist Party [CCP] and the People's Republic of China [PRC] since 1978. During that time he has never been the General Secretary or the Chairman of the CCP, nor China's Prime Minister or head of state. Indeed, since November 1989 he has officially retired from all his positions in the CCP and the government of China. Nonetheless he remains better known, both inside and outside China, than those who have been more formally appointed to positions of authority and few doubt that since the late 1970s he has been the single most important individual in China. Together with Mao Zedong and Zhou Enlai, Deng is usually regarded, with reason, as one of the key figures in the evolution of communism in China. Whatever else he may have achieved, more than anyone else it was he who was responsible for reversing the political and economic lunacy of Mao's later years, and for starting the process of bringing China into the twentieth century.

In the West, Deng has become famous in two different ways, with widely differing images. The first is as the capitalist world's favourite communist during the late

Deng Xiaoping

1970s and early 1980s. During those pre-Gorbachev years the CCP under his leadership abandoned the political strait-jacket Mao had imposed on the PRC during the Cultural Revolution, decided on a programme of modernization and instituted considerable political reforms. At times it even seemed that the CCP was prepared to abandon any pretence of communism. Both reform and modernization were based to a large extent on foreign economic involvement in China. There was an urgent need for China to improve its image abroad and its foreign relations. Deng Xiaoping was a key player in those efforts, speaking at the United Nations and touring the world, visiting the United States, Japan, Western Europe and South-east Asia at the head of government delegations. Appearing on television in a ten-gallon hat when in Houston did his and China's cause no harm at all. A short man with a round face, he projected a comfortable image like everyone's favourite uncle. For the United States government China under Deng seemed an appropriate ally in its strategic moves against the Soviet Union, and it was fully prepared to play the China Card. In 1985 Deng was even nominated as *Time* magazine's Man of the Year, the first time a communist had been so honoured.

All this changed rapidly in 1989. Deng is now notorious as the 'Butcher of Beijing,' the man responsible with Prime Minister Li Peng and Head of State Yang Shangkun for having sent troops into Beijing during May 1989 in order to suppress popular demonstrations. This confrontation between the population on the one hand, and the CCP and the government of China, on the other, came to a head on 4 June with the forced clearing of Tiananmen Square (where the demonstrations had been concentrated) by armed troops of the People's Liberation Army [PLA] and the subsequent considerable loss of life. Once again television has undoubtedly had a role to play for the events unfolded under the eyes of the international

Introduction

media whose reporters had gathered in Beijing, originally for the historic visit of President Gorbachev. Now Deng is seen as a tired, old man (he was 85 in the middle of 1989) out of touch with his own population, determined to hold on to power no matter what.

This political biography provides an explanation of the relationship between those two images of Deng. Both are over-simplifications, as must necessarily be the case. Any contradiction is more apparent than real. Deng has been a committed communist for all his adult life, and part of his adolescence. At the age of 16 in France he became involved with the people and organizations who were soon to form the Communist Party of China. From then on the party organized his life. It sent him to Moscow and back to China. At its direction, he travelled all over the country before the CCP came to power in 1949, working and fighting for the communist cause. Though the CCP may not have decided whom he was to marry, it certainly determined his marriage choices and his divorce. After 1949 Deng's commitment has led not only to high office, but also to persecution and vilification. In both 1966 and 1976 he was criticized and removed from his leadership posts. On both occasions, as when he had been disciplined in 1933, Deng accepted the need for party discipline to be maintained through the process of criticism and self-criticism – though not of course the conclusions of that criticism. He accepted party discipline as stoically as possible and waited for the opportunity to re-present his case.

Deng Xiaoping has also been a committed modernizer and nationalist, determined to make China both economically strong and politically powerful in international terms. In that endeavour he is often misleadingly characterized as a pragmatist. It is certainly true that he is no slave to dogma, and he clearly does not believe that all the truths of the successful road to socialist development are to be found in the works of Marx, Lenin or Mao.

Nonetheless he has a clear vision of the ways in which China's modernization should proceed and it is those ideas which have provided the opportunity for his opponents within the CCP to remove him from office. On each of the three occasions when he has suffered that fate his reaction has been to stick to his views and argue his corner while accepting party discipline.

Deng's vision of socialist development had its origins with Mao Zedong in the early 1930s in Jiangxi, and with the policies implemented by the CCP in Yan'an. It reached its first real manifestation during the Sino–Japanese War in Taihang as Deng attempted to adapt the Yan'an experience to the similar but different conditions he found there. In Jiangxi during the 1930s Mao had attempted to build a revolution in China from the countryside into the cities and from the bottom up. At that time Mao was not hidebound by dogma or overimpatient with the revolutionary cause. He realized it would take time to transform China and that what was required at each stage of the revolution would be maximum popular participation and support, as well as a sound economic base. Thus, for example, in the process of land reform not all the peasants should be dispossessed of land. Only the very richest should be made an example of and even then they too should be allowed to benefit from the land reform. The overwhelming majority – including middle peasants, who might be quite wealthy in relative terms – should certainly not feel threatened by CCP campaigns. In these ways Mao, and later Deng, had hoped to maximize both popular support and economic production. These principles, entailing slow but steady change, lay at the heart of Mao's later appeal to what was characterized during the 1940s as 'New Democracy' as the CCP prepared for national power under conditions of war. Indeed, they were even applied after 1949 for a while, until first Mao's impatience and then his personality became the main determinants of Chinese politics.

Introduction

In short, Deng has been pragmatic, rather than a pragmatist, with the ability to be more than a little stubborn once he has reached a decision. For Deng Xiaoping communism has been an organizational as much if not more than an intellectual response to the problems China has faced in the 20th century. What is required is a united China, strong leadership, and the energy of the Chinese people, all of which can only be provided, in Deng's opinion, by the CCP. It may well be that this vision is fatally flawed; nonetheless, it remains Deng's vision.

The Chinese tradition of biography is not the same as that which has become established in the West. Rather than a measured evaluation its purpose is largely didactic, the results tend to hagiography, and the methodological basis which is an essential part of Western biography is absent. Gossip, rumour and innuendo have traditionally been the essential staple of Chinese biographies. The Western tradition relies on personal memoirs; interviews with relatives, friends, and those involved with the subject in a professional capacity; and on documents, personal and public. Usually too it is considered good manners to wait until the subject is dead.

In this case there are no personal memoirs and interviews are not possible. The personal recollections of others, though they have increased during the 1980s, remain few and far between. Even the documentary evidence is somewhat limited, providing what information it does on Deng's activities and speeches, but almost nothing on his feelings and attitudes, most of which have to be inferred from his actions. Deng himself has explicitly discouraged his own biography – official or otherwise. The nearest any source published in China has come to an authorized biography has been a short essay included in a 1988 volume of Deng's life in photographs.[1]

This then is a political biography not simply because

Deng Xiaoping

Deng Xiaoping is primarily a politician and statesman, but also because of methodological constraints. Any attempt at psychohistory, for example, would face major problems. In any case, Deng's life is fascinating not simply in itself but also for the light it throws on the evolution and dynamics of China's politics, particularly within the CCP. Although Deng was not a major figure in the CCP leadership until the 1940s he was involved in the party's formative processes. After 1949 the story of his life is virtually the story of Chinese politics. Moreover, the dramatic rises and falls in Deng's political fortune not only require explanation, they clearly are more generally instructive about the processes of politics. There are few political systems – particularly those dominated by communist parties – which permit one individual found guilty of political crimes on three separate occasions not only to live, but to bounce back repeatedly, eventually to become the 'paramount' leader.

The emphasis on political biography means that most of this book is concerned with Deng's life after 1949, the period when he has been a central influence in China's politics. It ignores almost all of his early life before the age of 16, about which virtually nothing is known. However, it does not ignore the years between 1920, when Deng arrived in France, and 1949, for those were the formative years in which his later political career was grounded. During those years he was a party official, political organizer and eventually a very successful soldier. He formed the personal associations which ensured his political survival: notably with Mao Zedong, Zhou Enlai, and the CCP's military and political leadership in Taihang. He also developed his own particular vision of China's future as he sought to implement party policy in the border region centred on Taihang. He created one of the PLA's most successful armies from very unpromising material and, during the late 1940s and the civil war between the CCP and Nationalist Party, was

Introduction

responsible for two military engagements that led directly to CCP success in 1949. The first was when the army led by Liu Bocheng and Deng broke through the enemy lines which had them pinned down in the north and swept into central China. The second was the decisive Huai-Hai Campaign when the CCP forces finally defeated the Nationalist armies protecting the Yangtze and the Nationalist capital at Nanjing. Deng's close relationship with the PLA has been an important and recurrent theme in his career, particularly during and after the Cultural Revolution.

The remainder of this introduction provides the essential background to Deng's political biography. It details the little that is known about Deng's early life in Sichuan province, and contains an overview of Chinese politics and the CCP's history. One section deals with the CCP's path to power before 1949, another with the PRC during the era of Mao-dominated politics and a final section examines the important characteristics of inner-party conflict within the CCP that have helped determine Deng's career.

Family background and early life

Deng Xiaoping was born Deng Xixian on 22 August 1904 in Sichuan province, the heart of West China. Like many revolutionaries, Deng adopted a *nomme de guerre* which became common usage, in his case in 1927 when civil war between the CCP and the nationalists first broke out. Later, in 1929 when he went as a political organizer to Guangxi province he once again changed his name, if only temporarily, to Deng Bin. The China of Deng's childhood was very much a traditional society, governed more by the seasons and the requirements of farming than by the fast-decaying imperial system. Indeed tradition played such a role in everyday life that even when Deng reached France he still preferred to render his birthdate according to the Chinese agricultural calendar as 12 July (that is the 12th day of the 7th month) when he registered as an alien in Marseilles, rather than according to the Western Gregorian calendar.

Deng's family lived in Paifang village of Xiexing township in Guang'an County, some 100 kilometres north of Chongqing. Chongqing, the last major city upstream from Shanghai on the Yangtze and some 2500 kilometres from the sea has historically been a large metropolis. However, its hinterland, unlike other parts of Sichuan province such as in the west around Chengdu, has not been notably wealthy. Deng Xiaoping's father, Deng Wenming was a relatively prosperous farmer, a landlord who rented out his land and who worked for most of his later life as a minor official in the county government.

Deng Wenming was a Hakka and originally a native of Guangdong province in southern China who had moved to Sichuan well before Deng's birth. Hakkas, who speak a Chinese similar to that found in Fujian province in East China, are to be found all over the south, and have a reputation for being doughty fighters and for sticking together. However, as far as can be ascertained Deng Wenming became fully assimilated. Certainly Deng Xiaoping shows no particular evidence of his Hakka background through his father's line and speaks Chinese with a pronounced Sichuanese accent. Other characteristics of the Sichuanese are frequently used to describe Deng Xiaoping. For example, the Sichuanese are often described in terms of their food which is noted for being hot and spicy. The Sichuanese temperament is regarded as peppery – it has a short fuse and inflames quickly, but bears no grudge or malice when it cools down.

Deng Wenming's relative wealth was reflected in the size of his family. Altogether he had four wives and thirteen children, though not all of them his own – seven sons and six daughters. His first wife, Zhang, had no

Introduction

children. His second wife, Dan, had four boys and three girls. The third wife, Xiao, had a son; and the fourth, Xia Bogen, had a daughter from an earlier marriage, and two sons and two daughters. Deng Xiaoping was the eldest son though not the eldest child – having an elder sister, Deng Xianlie – of Deng Wenming's second wife, Dan. However, she died early in her children's lives and it appears that Deng had a closer relationship with his father's fourth wife, Xia Bogen. Years later when Deng Xiaoping suffered internal exile during the Cultural Revolution, Xia Bogen, by then old and infirm, accompanied Deng and his wife.

The fate of the members of Deng Xiaoping's immediate family is largely unrecorded, though it seems that when he could he tried to do his best by them. As just indicated he attempted to look after his step-mother Xia Bogen during the Cultural Revolution and spent a large part of that time in nursing her. One of Deng Xiaoping's younger brothers, Deng Ken, who was born in 1910 became a schoolteacher in Guang'an County, and then later a newspaper editor. He joined the CCP in 1941, went to Yan'an and worked in the nascent New China News Agency. In 1949 he became deputy mayor of Chongqing and later moved to a similar post in Wuhan. Criticized as a 'Capitalist roader' during the Cultural Revolution – no doubt a classic case of guilt by family association – he was later rehabilitated and was able to retire in 1982 when Deputy Governor of Hubei province.

Another of Deng Xiaoping's brothers was not so lucky. Deng Shuping, born in 1912, became head of the family on his father's death and a local official in the Nationalist Party – the CCP's opponents in the civil war. After 1949 he read law at university, and was appointed to positions first in Guizhou province (just south of Sichuan) and then in Chongqing. Under the pressure of criticism from Red Guards during the Cultural Revolution – presumably as much about his earlier career in the Nationalist Party as his relationship to Deng Xiaoping – he committed suicide in 1967. Deng Wenming died in 1938. His job as an official of the county government frequently took him far away from Guang'an. He had been in Chengdu but, anxious to be home, instead of sticking to the main roads from Chengdu to Chongqing and then from Chongqing to Xiexing he decided to cut across country. Not far from Guang'an he stumbled across a group of bandits, who promptly beheaded him.

In 1909 at the age of five, Deng Xiaoping started out on the traditional path to imperial service by being enrolled in a private preparatory school to be educated in the Confucian classics. However, with the collapse of the imperial system and the revolution which overthrew the Manchu (or Qing) dynasty in 1911 there was little point in continuing. Deng was enrolled instead in a primary school with a modern curriculum and later graduated to the middle school in Guang'an. Later, Deng's quest for education was to lead him first to Chongqing and then to France. There is no record of any particular reason for this move, and no suggestion of any disagreement with his family or parents. David Bonavia has argued that since Deng Xiaoping was the eldest son there would have been at least an expectation that he should stay at home and prepare to take his father's place after the latter's death.[2] This is possible but also unlikely in this family given that the next eldest son also did not assume the leadership of the family.

The early decades of the twentieth century were a turbulent time for China's intellectuals. They recognized the challenge to China posed by the Western imperial powers and Japan, and sought solutions to its problems. Though many of these problems had been caused during the 19th century by colonial incursions into Chinese territory, nonetheless there was a kind of love-hate relationship with the West and several Chinese reformers looked to the promotion of Western ideas and systems of

Introduction

education as a means of modernizing China and making it strong again. One of these was Li Youying, who had himself been educated in Montargis just south of Paris. In 1912, with the active co-operation of the Mayor of Montargis and several other French notables, as well as Cai Yuanpei, Li established the *Société chinoise d'Education rationelle française* to send Chinese students to France.

By 1919 many Chinese had gone abroad to study, and though the original intention of educationalists such as Li might have been that their parents should pay for their education, this rapidly proved impractical. Instead the Work-study movement was started – in Chinese it was called *Qingong jianxue*, literally 'diligent work, thrifty study' – whereby Chinese students abroad engaged in part-work, part-study. With the birth of modern Chinese nationalism in the May 4th Movement – so called because on 4 May 1919 students in Beijing demonstrated against the decision of the Versailles Treaty which instead of repatriating Germany's former colony in Shandong simply passed it on to Japan despite China's support for the allies in World War I – many young Chinese were attracted by the opportunity to travel and be patriotic at the same time.

Necessarily if Chinese students were to live in France they would have to learn French. In 1919 Wu Yuzhang, a member of the Chinese Revolutionary Party, opened a school in Chongqing to prepare Sichuanese students for France. Deng enrolled and engaged in his first political activity, albeit in a very low-key way. Together with his classmates he joined in a boycott of Japanese goods. In 1920 some 90 of the students in Deng's class were selected to go to France through competitive examination. Deng was one. On 11 September 1920 the group left Shanghai aboard the Messageries Maritimes liner *Porthos* bound for Marseilles. They arrived on 13 December 1920.[3]

Deng Xiaoping

The Chinese Communist Party and the path to power

At the same time that Deng Xiaoping was leaving China for Europe, discussions were under way that eventually led to the foundation of the CCP. The collapse of the imperial system under the weight of foreign encroachment and internal problems rapidly led to the breakdown of central authority in China. Increasingly power came to be wielded by local warlords rather than any central government. In the intellectual ferment that was the May 4th Movement it was inevitable that some Chinese should look for national salvation to the new communist state in Russia. Apart from anything else, quite quickly after coming to power in Russia, the Bolsheviks made encouraging noises to the 'oppressed peoples of the East' to unite against imperial aggression and colonialism. They promised to restore any Chinese lands ceded to the Tsars and to share ownership of the Trans-Siberian Railway, a branch of which ran through Mongolia to Beijing. They also offered organization, finance and advice through the Comintern, the Communist International, established by Lenin explicitly to create communist parties worldwide.

Various Marxist discussion groups had already been established in China, though the most important was undoubtedly that based on Beijing University, where the demonstrations of 4 May 1919 had been organized. Together with national salvation associations, self-help groups and study societies of various kinds there were sufficient numbers on which to build a communist party and, with help from Comintern organizers, this was founded in July 1921. At first the CCP worked closely with the much larger Nationalist Party under Sun Yat-sen. Both were essentially nationalist parties initially motivated by events in the 19th and early 20th century to restore China's dignity and integrity. Thus a first priority for both was national reunification and an end to

Introduction

warlordism. Moreover, the Comintern had also been responsible, at Sun Yat-sen's invitation, for reorganizing the Nationalist Party as a revolutionary organization during the early 1920s.

Relations between the Nationalist Party and the CCP were always a little strained, as indeed they rapidly became between the CCP and the Comintern. The sources of conflict between the Nationalist Party and the CCP were personal as well as ideological and political. While Sun Yat-sen was alive he managed to hold the alliance together. However, after his death in 1925 his successor Chiang Kai-shek increasingly saw the CCP as a threat, at the same time that he sought accommodation with most of the leading warlords. The two parties had not formed a two-party alliance, but had agreed instead that CCP members should join the Nationalist Party as individual members. This arrangement enabled the CCP not only to develop its influence and organization under the umbrella of the Nationalist Party but also to effectively subvert the cause of the Nationalist Party from within. Deng Xiaoping's return to China in 1927 was part of that strategy, for he went to work for the northern warlord, Feng Yuxiang, in Xian. The Nationalist Party became increasingly polarized over the issue of co-operation with the CCP. In 1927 Chiang and other figures in his wing of the Nationalist Party moved to attack the CCP openly.

The source of conflict between the CCP and the Comintern was that the latter, under Stalin's direction, saw its role and that of the CCP as an extension of the Soviet Union's foreign policy. Partly for that reason and partly because Stalin wanted to prove a point to Trotsky in their struggle for control of the CPSU, the Comintern directed the CCP not to breach the alliance with the Nationalist Party at all costs. When members of the CCP in Shanghai were being rounded up, they were supposed to hide their arms and disappear rather than resist. The

CCP's organization of the peasantry for land reform was instructed to leave Nationalist Party members and their families alone. It was at this time that Deng Xixian became Deng Xiaoping. As 1927 wore on and first Chiang Kai-shek's wing of the Nationalist Party and then the party's left wing both turned against the CCP; Stalin's policies were to prove all but terminal.

Stalin's need for success in China led the CCP, now expelled from the Nationalist Party, to attempt a series of uprisings in China's cities. The intention was that CCP troops, often no more than poorly organized peasants drawn from the only recently organized peasant associations, should take the cities and bring about the downfall of the National Party government. In the event the most successful of these uprisings managed to seize and hold Nanchang, the capital of Jiangxi province, for only four days at the beginning of August. The remainder were abysmal failures entailing considerable loss of life. Still the Comintern pressed its views on the CCP which staged an abortive uprising in Canton that threatened the very existence of the CCP as an urban force. Although CCP headquarters were located in Shanghai, where Deng now was, they were underground and by the end of 1927 the CCP's strength or what was left of it was now gathering in rural guerilla bases or 'soviets', as they were paradoxically termed.

The CCP almost did not recover from the defeat of 1927. From 1927 to 1935 there was a series of inner-party struggles for power, as well as repeated military offensives by the Nationalists under Chiang Kai-shek. Mao among others drew lessons about the importance of peasant-based revolution, of guerilla and mobile warfare, and of the need to politicize the peasantry with programmes of social and economic reform. As part of the policy of fomenting rural insurrection now adopted by the CCP, Deng Xiaoping was sent to Guangxi. However, support for the rural soviets such as those

Introduction

established by Mao first in the Jinggangshan and later in south Jiangxi around Ruijin was ambivalent. Others within the CCP (as for example Zhou Enlai) continued to cling to the party's proletarian perspective and urban insurrection was attempted again in 1930. Deng, for example, was ordered to leave his rural base in Guangxi and march on a number of cities, including Canton: a move which was totally impractical and rapidly abandoned after military defeat far from the appointed goal. Elsewhere the attempted seizure of the cities met with equally disastrous results as in 1927.

Leadership of the CCP now passed to the '28 Bolsheviks' or 'Returned Students Clique'. These were a group of Chinese students educated in Moscow who had been sent back under Comintern direction to lead the Chinese revolution. They recognized that the emphasis in CCP work had to shift from the cities to the countryside. However, they were not prepared to hand leadership of the CCP over to Mao and his supporters, who had developed the most successful rural base area, the Jiangxi Soviet. In 1931 they moved the headquarters of the CCP from Shanghai to Ruijin, the capital of the Jiangxi Soviet. Deng went too. Throughout these years Mao's more orthodox opponents criticized him repeatedly for his pragmatic views. Because of his success and popularity it proved impossible for them to remove Mao's influence altogether, but they nonetheless tried through attacks on his supporters and those who shared his views. In 1933, in one such campaign directed at Mao, Deng Xiaoping was removed from office by the CCP and disciplined.

Chiang Kai-shek meanwhile also posed a threat to the CCP. When he could turn from his problems with recalcitrant warlords and the increasing threat of Japanese invasion, he launched a series of military 'annihilation campaigns' against the various CCP rural soviets. Up to 1934 the CCP was able to hold out in the Jiangxi Soviet because of its guerilla warfare tactics and Chiang's other problems. However, in 1934 the Nationalist army adopted a new and highly successful tactic of blockade. At the same time the CCP under the direction of its Comintern advisers abandoned its guerilla tactics for those of positional warfare. The results were catastrophic and, staring yet another major defeat in the face, the CCP opted for the strategic retreat which became the Long March.

The Long March is justifiably famous for its heroism: in Edgar Snow's words it was 'one of the great triumphs of men against odds and man against nature'. Some 90,000 soldiers of the Red Army set off to they knew not where to find sanctuary. After a little over a year and marching more than 10,000 kilometres, the remnant, 5,000 or so, finally arrived at what was to become their destination in North China having fought off the Nationalist armies and crossed some of the most inhospitable terrain in the world, including 18 mountain ranges, deserts and marshes.

For the CCP, the Long March had three key political results. The first was that it essentially ended the internecine strife within the CCP which now became more or less united behind the policies of Mao and his supporters. The turning point actually came on the Long March at Zunyi in January 1935. The Comintern advisers were discredited and many who had previously opposed Mao (including Zhou Enlai) now changed their views. For those, like Deng, who had supported Mao the result was promotion. The second result of the Long March was that at its end in North China it presented the CCP with a secure base from which to expand, first at Baoan, and then later at the more famous Yan'an. By 1935 Chiang Kai-shek was once again embroiled in problems caused by warlords and impending Japanese invasion. The third result was that the Long March not only created a tremendous *ésprit de corps* among its survivors, it also created the legend of an invincible CCP and Red Army.

Undoubtedly a decisive turning point in the CCP's path

Introduction

to power was Japan's invasion of China in 1937. Under threat of invasion at the end of 1936 Chiang Kai-shek had been forced by his own generals to co-operate with the CCP once again. When the Japanese forces eventually advanced he retreated to Chongqing in the west, leaving the CCP entrenched in north China. From this position it was able not only to consolidate its position, but also to expand into the rural hinterland behind the Japanese lines and to become recognized by the population as the effective nationalist resistance. Following policies of rural mobilization, the CCP established first rural soviets, and then base areas and border region governments, as it could. Deng, for example, spent most of this time not in Yan'an but in the border region centred on the Taihang Mountains, where Shanxi and Hebei provinces meet. By the time of Japan's defeat the CCP controlled well over a quarter of China's population.

The end of the Sino–Japanese War saw repeated attempts to avoid confrontation between the Nationalists and the CCP, but these soon failed. In the ensuing civil war the CCP was successful not simply because they had developed a secure base and reputation during the Sino–Japanese War, but also because of the weaknesses of the Nationalist regime: morale was increasingly low among its troops, inflation was high and corruption was rampant. At the end of 1948 CCP forces won two decisive victories against the Nationalist Armies: one in the north-east, which threatened Nationalist control of north China and led to the surrender of Beijing; the other, in which Deng Xiaoping played a leading role, was for control of the Yangtze region and central China. By April 1949 CCP success was guaranteed.

Deng Xiaoping

The Mao-dominated era of Chinese politics

On 1 October 1949 Mao Zedong mounted the podium overlooking Tiananmen Square in the centre of Beijing to proclaim formally the establishment of the PRC. Though the CCP had after 28 years finally achieved national power, it faced enormous problems. The most urgent were to restore national unity, to bring inflation under control and to ensure the political control of the CCP, particularly in those areas where it had not been organized before 1949. As the communist armies gained control over the whole of China the device that was employed by the CCP to solve these immediate problems was the Military and Administrative Committee [MAC] – a body that not only brought temporary military rule but also allowed CCP cadres, most of whom like Deng had been soldiers for some considerable time, to become civilian officials. Each of the six major armies of the PLA came to dominate a region of China, and six MACs were established, one in each region. Deng was appointed the leading party cadre in the south-west, a region where the CCP had had little organizational presence before 1949.

In the early years of the PRC, the CCP was more concerned with consolidating its position than in implementing programmes of radical change. It remained committed to its revolutionary goals, but given the size of China's economic and social problems its outlook was gradualist. Land reform was introduced but in the urban areas capitalist enterprises were urged to continue operation and intellectuals were encouraged to co-operate with the CCP under an appeal to nationalism. Economic development and party expansion were the primary targets and, for the most part, they were successfully achieved.

Almost immediately after coming to power the PRC had allied itself with the USSR, though not enthusiastically due to the history of CCP–Comintern relations before 1949. Aid and advice were supplied by the Soviet

Introduction

Union, and the economic and political structures, as well as the policies adopted were designed, as they had been in Eastern Europe, to create a mirror age of the Stalinist state. By 1954, the CCP's consolidation of its rule was complete and these new structures were largely in place. China's economy, in particular its infrastructure, was to be governed by Five Year Plans. A new constitution and system of government had been established.

However, the Soviet model of development rested uneasily in a Chinese context and with the leaders of the CCP, for ideological, economic and political reasons. It was highly centralized, emphasized the development of heavy industry and addressed the needs of the cities rather than the countryside. The leaders of the CCP were not an urban, technocratic elite; and by the mid-1950s the command economy was beginning to result in shortages and bottlenecks around China. In addition, the Soviet model entailed an unequal growth strategy causing economic inequalities between China's different regions to increase. Perhaps most important, after Stalin's death, the CCP was increasingly unwilling to acknowledge the superiority of Soviet experience and leadership. By 1955, much to their advisers' disgust the CCP was beginning to look for an alternative 'Chinese road to socialism'. The Sino–Soviet split was not yet irreversible, but it was already in the making.

In the intra-party debates of the mid-1950s to determine what should replace the Soviet model, two broad views emerged which were to be at the heart of conflict within the CCP until after Mao's death in 1976. The more radical view was that of Mao Zedong who argued that growth should proceed as fast as possible in all fronts, fuelled by mass mobilization and enthusiasm. The more gradualist view, articulated by Chen Yun – who worked in economic planning from 1949 through to the 1980s and who was the economic architect of the 1978 reform programme – argued that China's economic development had to be slower, based on sound economic principles, and led by agricultural growth. At the same time, the measures which Mao took to argue his case and to get his own way had a considerable impact on Chinese politics, which from about mid-1955 on became increasingly dominated by his personality.

In mid-1955 the CCP had taken a gradualist approach to collectivization. Unhappy with the decision, Mao went over the heads of his colleagues in the leadership – and against the principle of collective leadership – to encourage provincial leaders to implement the first stage of collectivization ahead of party policy, before the end of 1955. Before long Mao was arguing that the First Five Year Plan could be completed in four years, a year ahead of time, and that the CCP should be bolder in its future plans. However, in the first three months of 1956 the economic results of Mao's over-enthusiasm became apparent, and to the extent that his strategy had been adopted, it was abandoned. The reversal rankled, and years later when reviewing these events Mao was highly critical of those who had made the decision. Those he criticized included Deng Xiaoping. Deng, having moved from the South-west to be a Vice-Premier in 1952, had by that time become a member of the CCP Political Bureau and Secretary-General of the CCP Central Committee.

At the 8th CCP Congress in September 1956, the party elected a new leadership including Deng as General Secretary (that is the leading secretary of the CCP and not just the secretary general to the CCP Central Committee) and adopted a definitely anti-Mao stance. Mao Zedong Thought as the guiding principle of the CCP was written out of the party constitution. Chen Yun's ideas for economic development became the basis of the Second Five Year Plan scheduled to begin in 1958.

However, Mao was not to be outdone. The Congress had agreed that a party rectification campaign was needed, not least to inform members of the change in

Introduction

line. Mao tried to force the pace by bringing forward the schedule for rectification, and by arguing that it should be carried out in accordance with his ideas on mass mobilization rather than in more orthodox ways. He wanted what he called 'extended democracy': the criticism of CCP cadres by everyone, regardless of their political affiliation, loudly and in public. In Mao's words: 'Let a hundred schools of thought contend, a hundred flowers bloom.' The experience would be good for the CCP, and would bind the CCP and intellectuals more closely together. Mao argued that because the CCP was now so well grounded in society, its exercise of power would be criticized but the fact of CCP rule would not be challenged. After much opposition within the CCP a rectification movement of this kind was launched in the so-called 'Hundred Flowers Movement' of May 1957. It was a disaster, with public denunciation of the CCP on almost all sides, and was quickly foreshortened and replaced equally quickly by a more orthodox rectification campaign aimed at severely disciplining those who had spoken out.

One of the mysteries of Chinese politics between 1949 and 1976 is why the remainder of the CCP leadership allowed Mao his head on so many occasions, even against their experience and judgement, and indeed even when it led to their own demise. Though he may have appeared god-like to the ordinary people, to those in the CCP leadership he was a colleague, if often a difficult one. They were originally a collective leadership who had come together and fought together during the pre-1949 struggle. One possible explanation goes back to the late 1920s and early 1930s when Mao had repeatedly been proved right and the majority wrong.

Despite the decisions of the 8th CCP Congress, at the end of 1957, Mao once again attempted to put his developmental ideas into practice. Through the offices of several provincial leaders an enormous mass mobilization campaign involving more than a quarter of China's peasant population was launched to improve irrigation. On paper at least the results were phenomenal and the Great Leap Forward in irrigation rapidly became a general economic Great Leap Forward. Mao's belief was that China could industrialize in 15 years by substituting labour for capital in investment. New, large-scale rural production units – the People's Communes – were established all over China in two months. Back-yard steel furnaces were started up everywhere. It was even claimed that communism – classless society – was literally just around the corner. Among all the other heresies, this was of course the one which annoyed the CPSU the most as relations worsened between the two parties, because as the first communist party state it assumed it would necessarily establish communism first.

By 1959 it became clear to some within the CCP that all was not well. However, when opposition to Mao's ideas came out into the open he responded by accusing his detractors, led by Peng Dehuai (the then Minister of Defence) of being counter-revolutionary. Partly as a result, the Great Leap Forward dragged on for another year but by the end of 1960 the economic situation was so critical that the CCP had no choice but to call a halt. Mao withdrew from the daily routine of government which he left to the head of state, Liu Shaoqi, the prime minister, Zhou Enlai, and Deng. In the aftermath, the CCP split between those who, like Mao, believed the strategy correct but flawed in its implementation and others, notably Liu and Deng, who believed the strategy to have been a disaster that should never be repeated. At the same time, the full emergence of the Sino–Soviet split left China isolated internationally. Nonetheless, in the first half of the 1960s under the gradualist strategy of Chen Yun, China successfully overcame the problems caused by the Great Leap Forward.

Mao, however, had not abandoned his ideas. More-

Introduction

over, through the early 1960s he increasingly came to believe both that he had been pushed out of political power and that the PRC had given up its commitment to revolution and would, if unchecked, move towards capitalism. In his view, politics rather than economics should determine China's development. This, if oversimplified, was the essential background to the Cultural Revolution which Mao launched in 1966. His target was the CCP itself, or at least its leading cadres such as Liu and Deng, who were castigated as 'capitalist roaders'. Mao turned for his support in launching the Cultural Revolution initially to the Red Guards, groups of politicized students, and to the PLA under the then Minister of Defence, Lin Biao. The Red Guards in particular were encouraged to overthrow all authority, to attack their teachers and almost all intellectuals, who were now criticized as the harbingers of counter-revolutionary values. With the support of Mao and a small group within the CCP leadership, now including Mao's wife Jiang Qing, they were wildly successful. Almost all officials of party and state were 'dragged out' and denounced; schools and educational institutions closed down; the more fortunate cadres and intellectuals who were not imprisoned, murdered, or who did not commit suicide, were sent down to the front line of production to learn the error of their ways among the toiling masses. This was to be Deng's fate: removed from power in 1966, he went into internal exile in 1969.

The result was near chaos, with order being maintained, where it was, by the PLA who consequently came to play a crucial political role in the unfolding of the Cultural Revolution. However, by the early 1970s the PLA's position in civilian politics was leading to further inner-party conflict only resolved with the death of Lin Biao and several other generals in an air crash over Mongolia. They were said to have plotted a coup against Mao, and when that failed to have fled to the USSR. It is

Deng Xiaoping

unlikely that the outside world will ever know the true story of the Lin Biao affair, or even where and when he died. Nonetheless, the removal of Lin Biao proved the opportunity for a rethink in the progress of the Cultural Revolution. In particular, it became clear that there was a shortage of administrative ability left to run China. The party and state had been purged during 1966–8; the PLA was being gradually returned to the barracks. Against the opposition of radical members of the CCP, more moderate leaders such as Zhou Enlai managed to have some of the victims of the Cultural Revolution restored to office. In 1973 one of these, and certainly the most significant, was Deng Xiaoping.

The remaining years of Mao's life were characterized by intense inner-party conflict. On the one hand, there were the radicals, who emphasized political goals and wanted to maintain what they saw as the achievements of the Cultural Revolution. On the other, there were those, notably Zhou Enlai and Deng, who stressed the need for economic modernization as a prerequisite to reaching the political goals of the CCP. In January 1976 Zhou died, and the resulting popular demonstrations in his honour and against the radicals provided an excuse for the latter to purge Deng once again. Hua Guofeng succeeded Zhou as prime minister, and when Mao too died, Hua also succeeded him as Chairman of the CCP having engineered a coup against the most extreme radicals in the CCP leadership, Jiang Qing and her three associates, the 'Gang of Four'. The way was paved for Deng to return to office, for a reversal of the Cultural Revolution, and for a determined drive to economic modernization.

Leadership politics in the CCP

Deng Xiaoping's repeated rise and fall from office has often puzzled non-Chinese observers, particularly those

Introduction

used to other communist party states where for the most part a purge is usually irreversible. Faced by this apparent enigma, some have tried to argue that Deng is more an administrator than a politician, who is able and willing to work with almost anyone. Bedeski for example, suggests that 'he is not a great political visionary. He is a fixer, an organizer, and a reformer.'[4] It is undoubtedly true that a major part of his political strength lies in his abilities as a fixer and organizer. On the other hand, although he may not be a 'great political visionary', as already indicated and as will become apparent later, he does have a relatively clear political vision. The explanation for Deng's intermittent career is to be found more in the nature of leadership politics within the CCP than Deng's adaptability.

An obvious starting point, and an important characteristic of leadership conflicts and their resolution within the CCP, is that purges in China have not necessarily carried the same connotation of blood and death which Stalin bequeathed to the Soviet Union and Eastern Europe. Indeed, though particularly during the Mao-dominated era of Chinese politics leadership conflicts frequently did result in violence and death, before the 1950s the CCP's tradition had been otherwise. Though this changed somewhat under Mao, the belief was always that leaders could be re-educated to see the error of their ways.

Whether entirely for this reason or not it is clear that in the history of the PRC it has been relatively common for former leading cadres of the CCP, the state administration, and the PLA who have fallen into disgrace to be recycled. Deng Xiaoping's case is clearly the most spectacular, but it is far from unusual. By the end of 1978 a considerable proportion of the leadership of all three political hierarchies that had been in office on the eve of the Cultural Revolution and which had been purged during 1966–8 had regained at least equivalent positions of seniority. Some leaders purged at the start of the

Great Leap Forward, for presumed or apparent opposition to Mao's ideas, were restored to office in the early 1960s, removed again in the Cultural Revolution and brought back again in either the early or late 1970s.

The excessive instability of Chinese politics from 1949 to the late 1970s was matched by an extraordinary leadership stability, not in terms of specific individuals but in terms of the relatively small pool from which those leaders were chosen. During those years the political line adopted by the CCP changed on average every four or five years. With each change came not only new policies, but also fresh organizational structures and personnel changes. However, the revolutionary generation which had fought together and won power in 1949 only relinquished its hold on the political system in 1985 when both biological and political factors became urgent considerations. Before that later date leadership changes incorporated few younger people, or those generally with different backgrounds and experiences. Remarkably this was the pattern even during the Cultural Revolution when one of Mao's stated aims was to bring in fresh blood to rejuvenate the leadership.

One explanation for this phenomenon lies with the age structure of the CCP leadership in 1949. When the CCP achieved power its leaders were in international as well as Chinese terms relatively young to be national leaders. Mao, for example, one of the eldest, was still only 54. Deng was 45. Consequently there was no need initially for them to train successors and there was no planned layering of potential leadership generations. By the time of the Cultural Revolution, some 17 years later, though there may have been an urgent need for successors, as Mao made plain, the issue became submerged in the wider conflict of the Cultural Revolution, which apart from anything else, delayed a solution still further.

A further explanation lies in the nature of factions and factionalism within the CCP. The leadership of the CCP

Introduction

since 1949 has been, and remains, highly factionalized. Individuals come together to provide mutual protection and assistance. Factional alignments may result from loyalty ties, career background, institutional affiliation, friendship, ideological perspective, attitudes to specific policy issues or personality. However, factions within the CCP are extremely fluid – not highly organized as, for example, in Japan's Liberal Democratic Party. Consensus and unity, rather than the divisions often associated with factions, are most definitely the order of the day for both traditional and contemporary reasons. The CCP has inherited a considerable portion of traditional Chinese political culture, not least that which emphasizes to a degree almost unimaginable in the West the requirement to maintain harmony. At the same time, the CCP's legacy from Marxism–Leninism is that the party is the correct interpreter of the one true ideology.

The size, number and complexity of factional alignments – some of which may be nested, others overlapping and cross-cutting – make decision-making very difficult, even within a relatively small body such as the CCP's Political Bureau. There is a need for individuals to build coalitions, but the process is almost impossible not least because no one wants to be on the losing side. This was particularly the case during the Mao-dominated era of Chinese politics because the punishments for being on the 'wrong' side could be so severe. Politics have therefore been both extremely conservative and brittle. Within the leadership there is an inbuilt tendency to maintain the status quo. Normally change is introduced experimentally and incrementally, in ways which may subtly pressure the leadership without seeming to threaten the balance of power. However, dramatic, sudden and more wide-ranging change also occurs not least when changes in the environment – for example, a major socioeconomic problem, a perceived external threat – or changes in the leadership itself, through death or illness, force a decision on the leadership and trigger rapid factional re-alignments.

In both 1966 and 1976, Deng's dismissals from office resulted from the brittle nature of Chinese politics. Both represented the rejection, at least temporarily, of his political vision. However, Deng's ideas do not provide an adequate guide to his career in Chinese politics. For individual leaders the relation between ideology or policy, faction and career has been far from clear. Policy changes may result from leadership changes but factions are rarely policy-based. Indeed members of a faction may not even share the same ideological perspectives or policy preferences. An illustrative example of the obvious confusion lies in the contrasting fates of Deng Xiaoping and Chen Yun during the Cultural Revolution. Of the two Deng had been more closely associated with Mao for some thirty years before the Cultural Revolution; Chen Yun's relationship though good was not quite as close. In the debates of the mid-1950s, Chen was the major voice in opposition to Mao's ideas on development; Deng was opposed to most of Mao's ideas, but prepared to give him support despite misgivings and at times spoke enthusiastically. In the Cultural Revolution both were criticized, but it was Deng who was purged as a 'capitalist roader', whereas Chen maintained a leadership position, if at a lower level.

The careers of individual leaders would seem to be determined more by loyalty ties than by their political ideas. Chinese politics are inherently personalist. Loyalty ties formed during an individual's career bind them to a specific leader or colleague. A major secret of Deng's success has been the extent of his network of loyalty ties, in many ways a function of his age. Politicized at the age of 16 he came into contact with some of the very earliest leaders of the CCP. Thereafter, through his involvement in different aspects of party affairs in different locations, he formed relationships which provided a wide network of

Introduction

support well up to the present. As a result, Deng, unlike some other leaders, could always find alternatives if one source of support failed him. He was old enough to be incorporated as a junior member of the leadership, and young enough to have had a longer and more varied active life in the CCP than most of the survivors of the revolutionary generation. Deng does not appear to have been overly ambitious in the way that Mao and Zhou both clearly were. Nonetheless, he was to grasp every opportunity with both hands.

Formative political years, 1920-49

1

The years from 1920 to 1949 not only saw the CCP's path to power, they also saw Deng Xiaoping's involvement and increasing importance within the party hierarchy. Deng's rise undoubtedly owed much to the friendships and associations he made during those years – and which were to prove of continuing significance once the PRC was established. Three in particular were to prove crucial. In France in the early 1920s and back in China again, on several occasions during the late 1920s and early 1930s, he worked with Zhou Enlai; in the Jiangxi Soviet during the early 1930s he first became closely associated with Mao Zedong; and in 1938 he first joined forces with Liu Bocheng in what was to become one of the strongest military and political partnerships for the CCP. For Deng the early Taihang years of that association were also to prove seminal in the evolution of his political vision. By 1949, though he had not yet achieved the national prominence of Mao Zedong or Zhou Enlai, he was on the verge of becoming a senior member of the CCP leadership. However, it had not all proved plain sailing either politically or personally, not least since he had been severely disciplined by the CCP in 1933.

Formative Political Years

Croissants, le Creusot and communism

Although Deng Xiaoping spent five years in France from December 1920 to January 1926 – from the age of 16 to 21 – there is little evidence that he became a francophile, at least politically, during those years. On the other hand, he did acquire a taste for French food and especially croissants. Prince Sihanouk, the former Cambodian leader exiled in Beijing, used to enjoy cooking French meals and would often send one round to Deng. Deng himself once confessed to Yang Shangkun that when he wanted to treat himself in Paris he would have a croissant with a glass of milk. Interestingly, it appears to have been Ho Chi Minh who instructed the young Deng on where to obtain the best of such delights. In 1974, on his first trip outside China since the Cultural Revolution Deng visited New York and was intent on buying some croissants until it was suggested to him that since he was returning to China via Paris he could do better there. This he did, buying a hundred which returned to China with him some to be duly supplied to Zhou Enlai and others, who had also formed the taste during their Paris days.[1]

As Deng's comment to Yang Shangkun appears to indicate, life was not easy for Deng or indeed the other Chinese worker-students in France. France in the early 1920s was in the middle of an economic crisis and work was hard to find. The Chinese rapidly found that their Chinese academic qualifications were not acceptable for entry to French institutions, and that their spoken French was really inadequate for study. Most tended to drift to Paris and those large industrial plants that employed large numbers of foreign workers, such as the Renault plant in Billancourt (a south-western suburb of Paris) where Deng worked for most of the last three years of his time in France. There they lived together in close proximity and many became involved in the nascent communist movement as much for social as political reasons.

The details of Deng's life before 1949 are hard to ascertain and this is especially true of his years in France. The most reliable source for his movements is his police record, though even then Deng only came under their relatively close scrutiny during 1925.[2] Nonetheless, it seems Deng spent the first half of his stay in France travelling around quite widely, taking work – including spells as a fireman on a locomotive and as a kitchen hand – almost as he could find it. From Marseilles he travelled to Bayeux where he enrolled in a secondary school for three months. During 1921, he worked at the Le Creusot Iron and Steel Plant in central France. Later in the same year he moved to La Garenne-Colombes, another south-western suburb of Paris, and worked in a factory. This was precisely the time and place that Zhou Enlai and three or four other politically active Chinese émigrés were establishing the Socialist Youth League of China – the forerunner of the CCP in France – though there is no direct evidence that Deng was as yet immediately brought into their orbit. Early in 1922 he finally arrived in Montargis, which must have been one of his goals when he had left Chongqing.

During the early 1920s Montargis – a pretty and genteel provincial town whose inhabitants would have been mightily surprised if they had known what was going on – played host to a series of Chinese radical worker-students. Chinese came not only from Sichuan but from other provinces too, including a significant number from Changsha in Hunan. They had been amongst the first to arrive in Montargis and had established a branch of the New People's Study Society which later became the nucleus for the formation of the Socialist Youth League of China. The New People's Study Society had been formed in 1918 in Changsha by Cai Hesen and Mao Zedong, and in 1919 had been active in

Formative Political Years

recruiting students to go to France. Mao stayed in China but Cai and many others went. These included Li Weihan, whom it seems reasonable to assume Deng met at this time, but who was to play a less benign role later in Deng's life. The Chinese attended the *Collège de Montargis* and many, like Deng, worked at Hutchinson's Rubber Factory.

On this occasion Deng stayed in Montargis for the best part of seven months. However, towards the end of 1922 he moved on again, this time to Châtillon-sur-Seine, where he attended secondary school. Early in 1923, he returned to Montargis, and for a much shorter time to Hutchinson's. His work record card notes not only that he was assigned to work in the boot and shoe-making workshop, but also that after March 1923 he was not to be re-employed.[3] There is no indication of what caused this remark though it is possible that Deng had fallen foul of tensions within the Chinese community because of his increasing involvement in political activities. Deng stayed in Montargis until June 1923, when he returned to southwest Paris and work as a fitter in the Renault factory in Billancourt, where he stayed until he left France in January 1926.

It is reasonable to assume that Deng's movements around France had some political motivation. (In 1936 Deng told Edgar Snow that he had been recruited to the CCP from the French Communist Party.[4]) Deng's organizational abilities had become clear at a very early stage. One of his colleagues on the trip from China recalled how when they reached Marseilles Deng took charge of arranging the Sichuanese students' disembarkation, with their luggage, while other Chinese were left not really knowing what to do. These organizational skills were soon to be engaged in political activities. In 1922, Deng joined the Socialist Youth League of China, which had been formed by radical Chinese then in France (as a precursor to the establishment of the European branch of the CCP) including Zhou Enlai, Cai Hesen and two sons of Chen Duxiu, the prominent Chinese Marxist and first leader of the CCP. In 1924 Deng joined the CCP.

Zhou Enlai was the editor of first the League's and later the CCP's bi-monthly newsletter and Deng worked with him, with responsibility for publishing it. In fact the documents and newsletters were simply reproduced, most often through hand-cut stencils and hand-rolled duplication. Deng's responsibility was as much practical as administrative, for he personally duplicated most of the league's, and later the CCP branch's, materials from then until he left France. When the Paris police raided his room on 8 January 1926, after he had left for the USSR, they discovered 'two oil-based ink printing kits with plates and rollers and several packets of papers for printing'. For these efforts his colleagues dubbed him, doubtless somewhat ironically but affectionately, the 'Doctor of Duplication'.

When Zhou Enlai left France for China in 1924 Deng took over his editorial responsibilities for the CCP newsletter *Red Light*. However, he was soon to become one of the more senior members of the CCP in France, and all this while still only twenty-one years old. In June 1925 a group of demonstrators organized by the CCP stormed the Chinese government's embassy in Paris in a purely symbolic gesture of solidarity with the party and workers in Shanghai. French public opinion was horrified and the action led to the deportation of some 50 CCP members and the voluntary return to China of about 50 more. Deng found himself elected as one of the new leaders of the party branch and as such came under close police scrutiny.

During the second half of 1925, Deng spoke on several occasions at meetings in the Paris area to promote the CCP cause or to discuss the current situation in China. One of these ended in a near-riot as opinions among the Chinese worker-students were highly polarized into pro- and anti-communist groups. It is reported that as the chairs flew across the room, Deng watched quietly from the platform. At another, five days before he left France, Deng argued strongly for a close alliance between the northern Chinese warlord Feng Yuxiang and the USSR. Strangely, within a little over a year Deng was to be appointed to work with Feng in Xian. The French police finally raided Deng's house in Billancourt on 8 January 1926. However, Deng and his companions had left for Moscow the day before.

Student to political worker

In Moscow, at long last, Deng Xiaoping was finally able to engage in further study. The path he followed from Europe to Moscow was one that had been well trodden by young CCP members and from the late 1920s on many Chinese were to study in Moscow. At first he attended the University of the Toilers of the East, and then later the Sun Yat-sen University. The latter had been founded in late 1925 – at a time of maximum co-operation between the CCP and the Nationalists – in order to train personnel for the revolution in China largely with funds donated by wealthy Nationalist Party members. It was an interesting time in the history of the CCP. Not only was there close co-operation between the CCP, the CPSU and the Nationalist Party, but the Chinese students themselves were caught up in the intra-party conflicts of the CPSU and courted by the followers of Bukharin, Stalin and Trotsky.

Among those Deng encountered in Moscow would have been Chen Shaoyu, more widely known since as Wang Ming, the most high profile of the '28 Bolsheviks' who dominated the CCP from late 1930 until early 1935; and Zhang Wentian, another of the same group. Among his classmates at Sun Yat-sen University were three of more than passing significance. One was Chiang Ching-kuo, the eldest son of Chiang Kai-shek, who himself was to become President of the Republic of China on his father's death, albeit when the Republic was confined to Taiwan. Another was Wang Jiaxiang, who returned to China as part of the '28 Bolsheviks', though perhaps more loosely associated than most. Wang was to prove an invaluable source of support to Mao in the latter's struggle for supremacy within the CCP in 1935, and was one of the main leaders (together with Mao and Zhang Wentian) of the Long March. In 1933 when Deng's career was under a cloud, it was Wang who provided immediate assistance.

A third classmate was Feng Funeng, eldest daughter of Feng Yuxiang. During 1926 Feng Yuxiang visited the USSR looking for aid and assistance. Feng Yuxiang was not a typical warlord; he was a Christian who maintained a highly disciplined army. Despite his fundamental anti-communism Feng was temporarily prepared to accept Soviet aid. However, Comintern assistance was made dependent on Feng joining the Nationalist Party and his participation in Chiang Kai-shek's military attempt to reunite China – the Northern Expedition – which was also supported by the CCP. Feng returned to China accompanied by about a hundred Comintern advisers, including several Chinese one of whom was Deng Xiaoping.

Feng Yuxiang's National United Army was based in Xian in north-western China. A military academy, dominated by several communist officers – until later in 1927 CCP members were all also members of the Nationalist Party – had been established there under the army's general headquarters, and it was Deng's intention to work there as a political instructor helping to train future communist officers. However, it was April 1927 and any such plans had to be rapidly dropped. The growing conflict between the CCP and the Nationalist Party came out into the open and Feng Yuxiang sided openly in this conflict with Chiang Kai-shek, rounding on his communist

Formative Political Years

officers and executing those of them who had not taken evasive action.

Deng went south to Wuhan, on the Yangtze, where he once again joined up with Zhou Enlai. Whether through that connection, or simply because he was around, Deng was appointed as a secretary to the CCP's Central Committee, currently headquartered in Wuhan. The Nationalist Party had split into two wings and the left wing had established its capital in Wuhan, away from Chiang Kai-shek's influence. It was a natural place for the CCP to establish its central secretariat for it seemed to offer some political protection.

Unfortunately, this calculation also went awry in July and August of 1927 when, largely as a result of Comintern interference, even the left wing of the Nationalist Party turned on the CCP, forcing it underground. The CCP Central Committee held an emergency meeting in Wuhan, which as a secretary (but not as a member with speaking or voting rights) Deng attended. The emergency meeting held General Secretary Chen Duxiu personally responsible for the party's catastrophe and removed him from office; adopted a new policy of military insurrection; and moved CCP headquarters secretly to Shanghai. Deng moved too, in the process changing his name to Deng Xiaoping.

In Shanghai, Deng, who was still only 23, was appointed chief secretary of the Central Committee. His responsibilities included looking after the CCP's central documents, confidential work, communications and financial affairs. It was a testing time for the CCP. In Shanghai and other urban areas CCP activities were almost totally underground. In 1927 and 1928 the CCP was engaged in a series of military insurrections, the most famous of which occurred at Nanchang in August 1927, but all of which were unsuccessful and expensive of human life and organizational strength. To cap it all the CCP itself was bitterly divided and was to remain that way for some time, as different tendencies within the party all struggled for control.

Little is known about Deng's activities during 1927 and 1928. In June 1928 the 6th CCP Congress was held in Moscow, both because of the situation in China and because the Comintern wanted to reassert its control. Most of the members of the new collective leadership of the CCP, including Zhou Enlai and Qu Qiubai, who had led the attack on Chen Duxiu, went to Moscow. However, the labour organizer Li Weihan, whom Deng had probably encountered in Montargis, stayed behind to manage CCP routine during the Congress, and Deng assisted him.

On a personal note, at the end of 1927 Deng met and married his first wife, Zhang Qianyuan. Little is known about her. (Her sister Zhang Xiaomei was slightly more famous, having been active in the Women's Federation and a member of the National People's Congress [NPC] during the 1950s and 1960s.) Unfortunately, the marriage only lasted eighteen months. Shortly after Deng left Shanghai for Guangxi, to foment insurrection, she had a complicated pregnancy and died.

Bose and peasant insurrection

By the late 1920s the CCP was dominated by Li Lisan, who aimed, at first at least, to follow the political line agreed at the 6th CCP Congress in Moscow. The peasantry were to be mobilized under CCP leadership: rural soviets were to be established and peasant uprisings were to be linked to urban insurrections. In line with these policies Deng Xiaoping was sent to Guangxi province, in Southwest China, in April 1929 to assist a minor warlord, Li Mingrui, who had communist sympathies, and Wei Baqun who had launched a peasant rebellion in the early 1920s. The journey to Guangxi was far from easy for both physical and political reasons. Once again Ho Chi Minh, who was living in Shanghai at the time and whom Deng had met in Paris, came to Deng's assistance. He advised Deng how to travel, to disguise himself as a businessman, and what other precautions to take en route. Under the *nomme de guerre* of Deng Bin, Deng Xiaoping set off first by boat to Hong Kong, then with the aid of the Indochinese underground communist movement by boat again to Haiphong in present-day Vietnam, then overland, re-entering China from the south-west. In those days it was not only the safest way politically, it was probably also the quickest.

The situation in Guangxi was not simple, and the CCP had been trying to expand its activities there for some years.[5] Deng was neither the only nor the first CCP cadre to be sent as a political organizer at this time: Yu Shaojie and Zhang Yunyi had preceded him during the previous two years. CCP support came from two different directions, a peasant movement and local army officers.

Guangxi is an area only half of whose population is ethnically Chinese. The rest belong to one of the many minority groups that populate China's south-western border with South-east Asia. Of these by far the largest minority nationality are the Zhuang, indeed they are the largest non-Chinese group in the whole of China, who account for about 35 per cent of Guangxi's population. For the best part of 1,000 years most of the Zhuang in Guangxi have been thoroughly sinicized, with the exception of those in the poorer and more remote areas around the Left and Right River Valleys in the province's north-west. Conflict was endemic between these remnant Zhuang and the rest of Guangxi and in the early 1920s the collapse of government led to the emergence of a self-protection Zhuang Peasant Movement based at Donglan to the north of the Right River under the leadership of Wei Baqun. Initially defeated by local landlords, Wei trained at the CCP's Peasant Movement Training

Institute in Canton before returning to Guangxi. This time the Zhuang Peasant Movement was more successful, forcing the provincial Nationalist Party authorities by 1926 to recognize its control of Donglan county. The leading Nationalist who dealt with Wei was also a member of the CCP, and he took the opportunity to recruit Wei and other peasant leaders. The Zhuang Peasant Movement was so well established that by 1927 when the Nationalist Party turned on the CCP it was able to survive.

The Guangxi Clique was an important factor in national politics during the mid-1920s not least because of Guangxi's army which was active well beyond provincial boundaries. Its leader Li Zongren was not only anti-communist but also not well-disposed towards Chiang Kai-shek. Nonetheless, many of its officers were left-inclined or members of the CCP. One of these was Yu Zuobo who with CCP approval engineered the officers' defection from Li Zongren to Chiang Kai-shek thereby not only enabling Chiang to defeat the Guangxi Clique but also bringing himself and another CCP sympathizer, Li Mingrui, to power in Guangxi. This was the situation Deng Xiaoping encountered in Nanning, the capital of Guangxi, when he arrived in 1929.

In Nanning Deng and Zhang Yunyi, a CCP veteran of the Nanchang Uprising in 1927, set about developing two brigades of pro-CCP soldiers, and continued Yu Zuobo's policy of sending aid and assistance to the Zhuang rebels in the Right River area. In September 1929 a CCP congress in Nanning agreed to establish a Red Army and to arm the peasantry. At the end of the month, Li Mingrui and Yu Zuobo were forced into battle against the reconstituted army of the Guangxi Clique, but without Deng and Zhang Yunyi who led their two brigades – some 1,000 men – up the Right River to Bose, not far from Wei Baqun at Donglan. Li and Yu were rapidly defeated, and Li retreated to Bose.

Formative Political Years

Bose is in the heart of one of the poorest areas of China. In the 1990s it remains economically backward and is one of six counties which receives special central assistance for that reason. In the late 1920s it was the major market for the local production of opium and by imposing a tax on the movement of opium through the town, but not curtailing its production, the CCP had access to an invaluable source of income. This revenue was used to pay members of the newly constituted 7th Red Army, and undoubtedly helps explain its rapid growth within a very short time to about 7,000 men.

In addition, in Bose the CCP adopted a programme of organization and peasant mobilization which brought rapid results. The local people and the new soldiers of the Red Army were to be politicized; the army was to be expanded and improved in quality as well as quantity; the peasantry was to be armed under CCP leadership; landlords were to have their property confiscated and land reform introduced. By December Deng, Zhang Yunyi, and Wei Baqun came together to declare the Bose Uprising and establish the Right River Soviet Government. Within a few months the soviet covered some twenty counties with a population of a million people. Deng, who was already the CCP's ranking secretary in Guangxi became the political commissar of the 7th Red Army.

Emboldened by success Deng went to Longzhou on the Left River and in February 1930 established a second soviet and the 8th Red Army. However, this enterprise was always much smaller, less well-organized and lacking in local support. The Longzhou Uprising was also much more violent than that in Bose. The French Consulate and the Catholic mission were both attacked because it was claimed that they were protecting rich landlords and merchants. The French responded by bombing Longzhou, and the border between Indochina and Guangxi was closed. Within two months the Longzhou Uprising was crushed by the Nationalist Army and the remnants of the

8th Red Army made their way to Bose.

However, even in Bose success proved to be much more illusory than at first had seemed to be the case. The Right River Soviet faced two major problems: it had failed to disarm its opponents and the local militias; and it had failed to politicize adequately. In particular, it had not recognized the importance of not being seen to behave as warlords did themselves – which was on the whole the local perception – not that the local Zhuang were likely to be as opposed to communist Chinese as they were to anti-communist Chinese. As the Right River Soviet tried to expand it found that when the Red Army moved on the landlords were able to reassert their authority and the *status quo ante* with little difficulty.

Deng had returned to Shanghai late in February for further instructions from the CCP leadership. When he returned to the Right River Soviet in August he found Bose and other towns had been lost. Moreover, the news he brought was not enthusiastically received for under Li Lisan's direction the CCP had adopted a renewed policy of urban insurrection and the 7th Red Army was ordered to leave its base and march on Liuzhou, Guilin (both in Guangxi) and Guangzhou (Canton). Unsurprisingly, there was a clash between the native Zhuangs under Wei Baqun, who wanted to disobey CCP orders and stay, and those like Deng, who though they must have found the orders impractical in the extreme nonetheless felt duty-bound to obey. In the event Deng, Zhang Yunyi and the majority of the 7th Red Army (some 20,000 men) set out for Liuzhou in September, leaving a small force behind under Wei Baqun. The soviet was attacked and collapsed almost immediately.

In October, Deng and Zhang Yunyi called a party congress of the 7th Red Army at Hechi en route to Liuzhou. Losses required that the army be reorganized and their goals reassessed. They decided instead to head for southern Jiangxi and the rural soviet established by

Mao. It was a long and tortuous journey which took them into northern Guangdong, back to Guangxi where Deng and Zhang became separated, and on to Jiangxi via Guangdong and Hunan, all the while harried by Nationalist armies. In February 1931 the 7th Red Army was reunited and took the county seat of Chongyi in Jiangxi. It had been a terrible precursor of the Long March that was to come. By the time the 7th Red Army reached Jiangxi it had been reduced to less than 4,000 men.

Jiangxi, Mao Zedong and the Long March

Once the 7th Red Army reached Jiangxi, Deng Xiaoping left Zhang Yunyi in command and headed for Shanghai. There he met up again with Zhou Enlai and those with whom he had worked before he had left for Guangxi, and wrote a report on the Bose Uprising. By this time Li Lisan had been replaced as leader of the CCP by the '28 Bolsheviks' – some of whom Deng would have known in Moscow. Although the new leadership was reluctant to acknowledge that Mao was in fact pursuing a more sensible, if gradual, revolutionary path in Jiangxi, they nonetheless recognized that Jiangxi was now the centre of CCP activities and in the first half of 1931 resolved to move party headquarters there. To that end Zhou Enlai, who had characteristically survived Li Lisan's purge despite his own close association, was appointed director of the Central Bureau for Soviet Affairs, one of whose tasks was to oversee the transfer of personnel to Jiangxi over the next two years.

In the middle of 1931 Deng Xiaoping was transferred to Jiangxi, and it was here that he first came into close contact with Mao Zedong, through his appointment as party secretary of Ruijin county. There is no substantive record of Deng's view of Mao's peasant policy at this

Deng Xiaoping

time. However, Deng's pragmatic outlook cannot have failed to be impressed by the contrast between southern Jiangxi and the events in the Right River Soviet. Certainly, later when Deng was responsible for the Taihang region during the Sino–Japanese War and the mid-1940s the lessons of politicization, production and guerilla warfare were repeatedly emphasized.

On the other hand, Deng's first contact with Mao could well have been confrontational. When Deng first arrived in Ruijin, he found many party members awaiting execution. A mutiny had broken out against Mao among an army group loyal to Li Lisan in southern Jiangxi at the end of 1930. Mao acted ruthlessly in putting it down and executed several thousand party members, who were castigated as belonging to a Nationalist Party secret organization designed to undermine the CCP. One consequence was a witch-hunt in which many other loyal CCP members uninvolved in any way in the dispute with Mao and certainly not engaged in anti-CCP activities came under suspicion. Deng acted promptly to end the hysteria: all cases were examined according to party rules, and those unfairly accused released. When Zhou Enlai arrived in Ruijin towards the end of the year he fully endorsed Deng's actions.

Deng's appointment in Ruijin did not last long. As more personnel were transferred into the Jiangxi Soviet Deng was moved aside for more senior cadres. He moved first to Huichang county and was given responsibility for the three adjacent counties of Huichang, Xunwu and Anyuan, though only the first of these was genuinely under CCP control. However, the move did have its compensations. One of the CCP officials in Huichang was the beautiful and energetic Jin Weiying, whom he married.

As 1932 progressed it became clear that Deng Xiaoping had become an energetic supporter of Mao's policies and that a good relationship had developed between them. He became director of the Propaganda Department of the Jiangxi CCP Committee during the year, but this too was to be a short-lived appointment. This time, however, the reason was political disgrace. As already indicated, there was considerable tension within the CCP between Mao and his followers on the one hand, and the '28 Bolsheviks' and their followers, on the other. As the latter moved into Jiangxi they tried to oust Mao and his followers from positions of authority and to minimize his influence politically. They opposed his views on guerilla warfare, argued that local armed forces should be disbanded and that a single powerful united Red Army should be created, and were dogmatic that land reform should dispossess former rich and middle peasants as well as landlords.

Presumably because of his experiences in Guangxi, as well as later in Jiangxi, Deng Xiaoping found himself in opposition to the CCP leadership on almost all counts. In particular, he argued that it was necessary to pursue a lenient policy towards the relatively prosperous peasants both to ensure that the CCP had sufficient support to ensure it could implement land reform and because as a guerilla force the CCP required a sound economic base for its own sustenance. In 1933 the CCP leader of Fujian province, Luo Ming, who had been an associate of Li Lisan's, was criticized by one of the '28 Bolsheviks' for being too negative in his attitude to mass mobilization. In fact he had simply pointed out that those living in border areas could not be mobilized endlessly with promises of future glory, however sympathetic they might be to the CCP: repeated enemy attacks were sapping morale. This was the time of Chiang Kai-shek's Fourth Encirclement Campaign against the Jiangxi Soviet. The CCP leadership took the opportunity to attack Mao and his supporters for their views, linking them to what they regarded as Luo Ming's defeatism, the so-called 'Luo Ming line.'

The attack on the 'Luo Ming line' started with an

article in the party newspaper in April 1933 by Li Weihan whom Deng had known in France and worked with in the Central Committee. Mao could not be criticized by name but others were, notably Deng, Mao Zetan (Mao's third brother) and Tan Zhenlin (who was to work closely with Deng from the mid-1950s until the mid-1980s). The attack continued with an article in the May edition of the party's journal *Struggle* when Li Weihan called for 'an attack without mercy and a struggle with brutality' against the miscreants. He certainly had his way, for Deng lost his position, was imprisoned and interrogated. He reportedly wrote two or three self-criticisms, or confessions, and when these failed to satisfy he characteristically dug in his heels saying 'I cannot write more. What I say is true.' In addition, Deng also lost his wife Jin Weiying who divorced him to marry Li Weihan. Whatever may have been the relationship between Mao and Deng before these incidents, afterwards it is clear that a strong political bond had been formed.

While he had been imprisoned and underfed, food had been smuggled in to Deng by Wang Jiaxiang, a friend from Moscow days, and his wife, and it was Wang who again helped Deng after the latter had been posted in disgrace to the Nancun district CCP committee in Le'an county in 1934. Deng spent only some ten days in Nancun before Wang had him assigned to the General Political Department of the 1st Front Army which Wang headed. Deng was appointed secretary-general to the department and worked in the Propaganda Division where his main task was to edit the army's official journal *Red Star*. It was a task he was to maintain right throughout the Long March.

The detail of Deng's participation in the Long March is sketchy to say the least. Partly this is because when the Long March started he was in semi-disgrace and partly because he later developed typhoid, from which he was

Formative Political Years

seriously ill by the time the CCP reached north Shaanxi. The turning point in Deng's fortune and, indeed, the CCP's was the Zunyi Conference in January 1935 at which the leadership of the '28 Bolsheviks' was overturned, and Mao's policies adopted. Shortly before the Long March started in October 1934 Deng was once again appointed chief secretary to the CCP Central Committee. Though it was a mark of Mao's ascendancy Deng was still not fully rehabilitated: a junior colleague remembers walking with him as far as Zunyi but not afterwards. Deng was present at the Zunyi Conference, presumably in his capacities as editor of *Red Star* and as chief secretary to the Central Committee. However, there is no record that he said a word at the meeting, simply sitting to one side, no doubt entirely satisfied by the proceedings. Later in the Long March when the Red Army was reorganized he was appointed to head the Propaganda Division of the Political Department of the First Army Group.

Taihang

When the Red Army arrived in northern Shaanxi in late 1935 it set about strengthening its much-weakened resources. A rural soviet had existed in the area since the late 1920s and this was now developed, later moving its capital to the more famous Yan'an in January 1937. Recovered from his illness, in the first half of 1936 Deng participated in the Red Army's expedition to Shanxi province, and then was appointed Deputy Director and later, Director of the Political Department of the First Army Group. In 1937 the Red Army was reorganized as the 8th Route Army, as a result of the agreement between the CCP and the Nationalist Party to co-operate to resist the Japanese. Deng was appointed Deputy Director of its Political Department, but it was an appointment he was only to keep until the end of the year.

Deng Xiaoping

At the beginning of 1938 he became the Political Commissar to Liu Bocheng's 129th Division, and Deng and Liu Bocheng were to co-operate closely and successfully for the next 14 years. In the Sino–Japanese War they expanded the 129th Division, and established and developed the Taihang Border Region. In the mid-1940s they created the 2nd Field Army of the PLA from the 129th Division and led it to victory in the civil war against the Nationalists. During 1949 to 1952 they established and organized CCP rule in China's Southwest region. First in Taihang as the ranking political cadre and military organizer and then, after 1947, as a soldier in the field this was to prove a seminal period in Deng's life.

Given Deng's relative lack of experience the extent to which he spent time away from Yan'an and, more generally, CCP headquarters during those years was quite remarkable, and presumably reflects the degree of trust placed in him by Mao Zedong. Even in 1942 and 1943 when Mao and his supporters finally stamped their control on the CCP and 'sinicized' the Chinese communist movement, Deng was not required to return to Yan'an for the rectification campaign. He only visited Yan'an four times: in September 1938 for an enlarged CCP Central Committee meeting; in July 1939 for an enlarged meeting of the CCP Political Bureau; in June 1945 for a meeting of the CCP Central Committee to which he had just been elected; and in August 1939 to marry Zhuo Lin, whom he had met the previous month.

The institution of political commissar was one that the CCP had inherited from the experience of the CPSU, which in trying to create the Red Army after the Russian Revolution recognized that many of the soldiers would not be committed communists and so required both political education and control. For the CCP the work of the political commissars and the political departments was somewhat different. It was their task not only to politicize and propagandize within the army but also among the civilian population. Indeed under the conditions of guerilla warfare this was a crucial responsibility for the CCP cause. In border regions, where the CCP was not well-established and enemy attack always likely – as where Deng operated for almost all 12 years – the army required the support of the local population to survive. In a very real sense there was no difference between army and party – CCP members had to be peasants by day and soldiers by night. Deng was thus responsible for political affairs within the military, and the ranking party cadre in the region. Indeed, when the CCP Central Committee established its Taihang Bureau, Deng's status was recognized by his appointment as secretary, the highest ranked position.

Liu Bocheng, like Deng was a Sichuanese. Born in 1892 he had a distinguished military career, despite losing one eye, before joining the CCP in 1926. When the CCP 8th Route Army was formed in 1937 he was given command of one of its three divisions, the 129th, which took up position in the Taihang Mountains, south-west of Beijing, and in a strategic position for movement between north and central China. Even before Deng's arrival Liu had carried out successful raiding parties against Japanese troops and aircraft. However, that was in the early part of the Japanese advance and as the year progressed and the Japanese occupied the cities of northern China, the Taihang region rapidly found itself the major CCP base behind enemy lines – Zhu De even moved the general headquarters of the entire 8th Route Army there.

Once the Taihang Revolutionary Base Area had been provided with sound economic and political foundations Deng and Liu immediately set about establishing others close by. Army units were sent out to mobilize the peasantry, organize them to resist the Japanese and establish local governments. Altogether another four base areas were initially established: in the Shanxi–Hebei–Henan and Hebei–Shandong–Henan borders, and the Southern Hebei and Taiyue base areas.

Despite these preparations, for most of 1940 the 129th Division was engaged in more positional warfare. Its first opponents were the Nationalist Party's forces stationed locally. Despite a formal United Front between the CCP and the Nationalists after 1936, conflict between the two was not uncommon. Friction finally exploded in 1940 and led in March to the withdrawal of Nationalist Party troops from the region. Later in the year, the 129th Division participated along with other CCP forces in the Hundred Regiments Campaign against the Japanese in north China which severely disrupted the Japanese lines of communication. However, one important result was that the Japanese now turned their military attention fully on the CCP border regions.

The 129th Division and its base areas and border region rapidly found themselves blockaded by the Japanese. Their eventual success in resisting repeated attacks, and indeed expanding their area of control during the remainder of the Sino–Japanese War owes much to the political and organizational skills of Deng Xiaoping. A border region government had been formally established in 1941 and by 1942 the areas under Deng's command were not only secure but had successfully developed their own temporary political and economic systems. It was no utopia but particularly in the middle of war, a military and economic blockade imposed by the Japanese, and severe natural disasters – including drought, famine, and plagues of locusts – it was quite an achievement.[6]

The Taihang region, for example, was by 1942 largely self-sufficient in everything except salt and matches, and was even exporting some manufactured goods. The border region government had its own tightly regulated credit and monetary system (including the issue of banknotes) and raised its own taxes. Indeed so successful were its financial policies that in 1943, taxes fell by almost a fifth. One interesting aspect of the taxation system, and a parallel with the reforms Deng introduced in the 1980s, was that individuals were taxed according to their average production in previous years and allowed complete control over any surplus.

Deng's policies in Taihang clearly drew their inspiration from the CCP's Yan'an experience. However, the attempt to adapt the 'Yan'an Way' also led to differences for conditions in Taihang were not identical, and in at least one case led to policy initiatives being taken up in Yan'an. Yan'an was a relatively small, single political unit deliberately created as a model for the CCP's expansion. The border region centred on Taihang was much bigger, with a fluctuating population, depending on the stage in the war, of between 8 and 30 million, but averaging about 16 million genuinely under its jurisdiction. The Taihang Revolutionary Base Area alone had about five million inhabitants. In contrast, Yan'an had a steady population of 1.4 million and was never invaded by the Japanese.

Taihang was less homogeneous socially; less certain and more changing in its area of occupation; and more genuinely behind enemy lines. A lower proportion of its population was under arms than in Yan'an; and it contained several base areas, some of which had for a while been controlled during the late 1930s by Nationalist forces. It was also economically much more complex, not least because of the degree to which it was engaged in economic warfare with the Japanese. The region was notorious for its poverty, and largely in consequence Deng directed the 129th Division almost from the start to engage in its own economic production rather than depend on the local peasantry for its supplies of provisions. This policy was not adopted in Yan'an until a few years later.[7]

Deng's report of July 1943 on economic reconstruction in the Taihang region is not only a model of the philosophy behind the CCP's successful guerilla strategy –

emphasizing the key relationship between economic production, politics and military victory – it is also a taut summation of Deng's later ideas on progress in general, and a paradigm of his economic pragmatism. Social transformation can only come gradually, and then by showing people that whatever policies are being implemented serve their economic, as well as their political interests. Socialism requires organization and economic might, and can only be built on 'capitalistic production'. (This phrase has been edited out of the 1989 official version of the report, published after the Beijing Massacre of that year, doubtless so that there should be no possible confusion as to the context of Deng's remarks or his intent.) Unlike Mao, Deng was not generally given to rousing rhetoric. Nonetheless his report finishes – 'Warfare, production and education are the three main tasks in the fight behind the enemy's lines. We are fighting for nothing less than complete victory. Production guarantees that victory, and education serves both production and armed struggle. The unity of all three is an unconquerable force.'[8]

If Deng's experience in Taihang shaped his ideas about the politics of change, it also provided him with the connections which were to ensure that he would have the opportunity to put those ideas into practice more generally. The roll call of those who served under or alongside Deng in Taihang – even excluding those who were part of the 8th Route Army's headquarters which was also based there – is an impressive section of the CCP's post-1949 leadership. For example, of the 87 individuals who served as members of the CCP's Political Bureau between 1949 and 1989, 17 had served in that border region. By way of comparison, 16 had been based in Yan'an during 1937 to 1945.[9]

A substantial number of those who had been with Deng in Taihang were to play significant roles in implementing reform during the 1980s. One of those was Bo Yibo, the former Vice Chairman of the border region government, who opposed Mao's ideas on economic development when a member of the CCP Political Bureau during the 1950s, and who co-operated with Deng during the early 1960s to mitigate the worst effects of the Great Leap Forward. Another was Zhao Ziyang, who met Deng for the first time in 1938 when he was a party secretary in his native Hebei–Shandong–Henan border area. Some sources report that Hu Yaobang (whom Deng had already, presumably, met in Yan'an in 1937 when Hu had been a student at the Resist Japan University and Deng had lectured there) was yet another, having become a political commissar under Deng in the Taiyue base area during 1942 to 1945. This is unlikely and the confusion probably arises because Hu later joined troops who had served under Deng in Taihang, and was himself part of the PLA's 2nd Field Army led by him and Deng. It is more likely that Hu spent all the years of the Sino–Japanese War in Yan'an as the Director of the Organization Department of the Military Commission of the CCP Central Committee, a position which brought him into regular and close contact with the commanding officers of all the CCP's military regions, including Liu and Deng. These considerations apart, the relationship between Hu and Deng certainly became close. Hu had recruited Deng's wife-to-be Zhuo Lin into the CCP in 1938; served under Deng in Southwest China during and after 1949; and became the Secretary of the Young Communist League under Deng in the mid-1950s.

The civil war

By the end of the Sino–Japanese War, the 129th Division had become a substantial army, soon to be reorganized as the Central Plains or 2nd Field Army of the PLA. In the manoeuvrings that accompanied the false attempts at a negotiated settlement between the CCP and the

Nationalist Party, Liu and Deng were able to defeat Nationalist Armies at the Battles of Shangdang and Handan. Nonetheless, were the Nationalist Army to move north and east to defeat the CCP because they occupied a strategic position, they were always going to be a first target in the coming civil war. Chiang Kai-shek moved troops to northern Shaanxi and Shandong surrounding Liu and Deng in what the latter described as a 'dumbell strategy'. However, rather than waiting to be squeezed, Liu and Deng (to the Nationalists' surprise) made a bolt for the south in June 1947. The aim was to reach the Dabie Mountains, between Nanjing and Wuhan north of the Yangtze. Such a position would be relatively easy to defend and provide the CCP both with control of the central China plains and a vantage point to attack the nationalists along the Yangtze.

Despite the element of total surprise the strategy almost failed. The terrain was barely passable, because of mud and marsh, and after a 28-day battle to break through the initial encirclement the army undertook a 20-day 500 kilometre forced march to safety. For a full army this was no mean feat and something of a gamble, particularly since they could not secure a retreat. The decisive battle on the march was at the crossing of the Ru river, which was nearly a disaster as the army came under enemy artillery fire. Undoubtedly success here ultimately owed much to both Liu and Deng, who not only personally led the march on foot but continually exhorted their tired troops to greater feats of heroism.

The occupation of the Dabie Mountains had several consequences for the 2nd Field Army. It allowed them time to recuperate and rebuild; it allowed them to occupy a sizeable proportion of the Nationalist Army that might have been fighting the communists elsewhere; and it allowed the CCP to use its superior strategic position to plan a final campaign in the south against the Nationalists. That final campaign – the Huai–Hai campaign, so called because it took place between the *Huai* River and the sea (*hai* in Chinese) – centred on Xuzhou and was coordinated by Deng Xiaoping, who brought together Chen Yi's 3rd Field Army with the forces of the 2nd Field Army. In a classic encirclement, often cited by military historians as one of the greatest land battles of the twentieth century, the CCP destroyed a Nationalist Army of half a million men between November 1948 and January 1949.

Together with CCP victory in the north-east and the surrender of Beijing, success led directly to national power in 1949. The CCP army, with Deng as leading secretary of its East China Bureau, crossed the Yangtze in April 1949 taking Nanjing, Shanghai and the surrounding provinces and directly causing the Nationalists to leave the mainland for Taiwan. Undoubtedly Deng's roles in both the Huai–Hai campaign and the drive on the Dabie Mountains have been overstated for contemporary political reasons by Chinese historians during the 1980s. Without doubt, though, his military as well as his political contributions were real enough. Certainly, by late 1947 members of the Central Plains Field Army had already decided that it was now Deng, rather than Liu Bocheng, who was the senior of their two leaders. Not that there was any rivalry between the two, for right from when they first came together in 1938 it seems they liked each other immensely and formed a long-lasting friendship. However, it was not just Liu's personal support that was to prove so important to Deng in the future, but rather the network of relationships he had developed within the CCP's military and political leadership.

General Secretary of the CCP, 1949–60

2

With the establishment of the People's Republic of China (PRC) in 1949, Deng Xiaoping came to national prominence, first as the party leader of the South-west Region, and later as Vice-Premier of the government, secretary to the Central Committee, and then General Secretary of the CCP. By 1956 and the 8th Congress of the CCP, Deng was the fourth-ranked of the party's leaders. When the Great Leap Forward was called to a halt at the end of 1960, he and Liu Shaoqi were given the prime responsibility, by the CCP and by Mao, for the future direction of the party and government. Deng's politics during this period are most often portrayed in one of two ways: either as Mao's man, whom the latter brought into the leadership and could rely on; or, particularly in and after 1956, as one of those coming into increasing conflict with Mao over the latter's vision of China's future. Both characterizations are misleading. Mao clearly did think of Deng as a capable and loyal supporter. However, if Deng was anyone's other than his own he was the whole party's. During these years Deng's actions were motivated by his emphasis on party unity and party discipline, rather than his personal support for or opposition to Mao. It was that motivation which first brought him Mao's praise and then later led him into increasing conflict with the Chairman.

Regionalism

At the end of 1949, and after the celebrations attending the establishment of the PRC in October, Deng and Liu returned to lead the 2nd Field Army in its advance on the South-west Region – the provinces of Sichuan, Yunnan and Guizhou – from the east. Its task, in co-operation with part of the 1st Field Army moving in from the north, was to complete the CCP's victory, which was duly achieved by the end of the year, meeting very little resistance. For Deng personally, it meant the first family reunion since he had left home in 1920, and he set up house in Chongqing with his brother Deng Shuping, his elder sister, Deng Xianlie, his sister-in-law (married to a younger brother) Xie Jinbi and his father's fourth wife, Xia Bogen. Professionally, he had been appointed the 1st secretary of the CCP in the South-west Region and now officially outranked Liu Bocheng, who was his deputy.

During the first five years of the PRC, and particularly until late 1952, politics and government were highly regionalized. The South-west Military and Administrative Committee, which Liu and Deng headed, like its counterparts in China's other five regions was a temporary measure designed to start economic reconstruction, provide political stability, and consolidate the position of the CCP. Deng's organizational skills and political perspectives were very much in evidence during those years. The Southwest faced three particular tasks. Because it had been the last region to be conquered as the PLA swept through China from the north, the remnants of the Nationalist armies which had been swept before it were concentrated in the region and were either forced to surrender or turned to banditry. Altogether the

Southwest was left with some two million government dependents, including not only former Nationalist soldiers but also former government officials who had fled from other parts of China. Deng's solution was to disperse those displaced as quickly as possible, and to ensure a steady supply of homes and jobs in order to meet their immediate needs and to make banditry less attractive. Nonetheless, where bandits continued they were met with force.[1]

A second task facing the Southwest more seriously than elsewhere was to combat the weakness of CCP organization. The CCP had almost no experience or organization in the Southwest before 1949 and few members. Recruitment was a major priority, but even the speed with which that was achieved brought further problems as it adversely affected the quality of leadership, leading to a need for immediate rectification, not least to instil party discipline; something Deng was to become preoccupied with during the 1950s.

A third and similar problem was that of the minority nationalities. The Southwest has a higher proportion of non-Han Chinese than other regions. Relations between the minority nationalities and the Han Chinese were traditionally poor and the CCP had few native cadres. In addition, the CCP considered many aspects of their social structures to be both feudal and antagonistic to the CCP's goals. In addition to a policy of positive discrimination towards non-Han administrators and CCP recruits, Deng exempted those areas where they were concentrated from participation in national political campaigns – such as land reform – until other more fundamental social reforms – the abolition of slavery, for example – were completed.

On the whole, regionalism was not a problem. A regional system of government had been adopted as a temporary measure, and the leaders of the six large regions were appointed primarily because they had held

General Secretary of the CCP

military positions in the CCP armies at the end of the civil war with the Nationalists. If they happened to serve in their native region, as was the case with both Deng and Liu, it was a happy coincidence that may have helped make them that much more acceptable to the local population, not least because they were literally able to speak the same language. In 1952, when the CCP started the process of recentralization there was no apparent resistance. Liu became Director of the PLA Military Academy in Nanjing (he was 60 by this time) and Deng became a Vice-Premier of the Government Administrative Council (later under the 1954 State Constitution, the State Council) and for a short time a member of the State Planning Commission and the Minister of Finance.

There was, however, a regional dimension to the major political crisis of the early 1950s, the resolution of which was to play an important role in Deng's career. In a series of events that have been shrouded in mystery until relatively recently, Deng's regional counterparts in Northeast and East China – Gao Gang and Rao Shushi respectively – were first dismissed from their posts in the leadership (in early 1954) and then expelled from the CCP altogether in 1955.[2] In addition to their regional posts Gao was Chairman of the State Planning Commission and Rao Director of the Organization Department of the CCP. Both were in favour of recentralization, and the real source of conflict was ambition. Gao, who took the initiative, wanted to replace Liu Shaoqi (Vice-Chairman of the CCP) and Zhou Enlai (Premier) in the hierarchy, and particularly the former as Mao's deputy and presumed successor.

Emboldened by what he presumed to be Mao's favour and support, Gao Gang actively campaigned against Liu and Zhou. He portrayed them as anti-Soviet, whereas he had good relations with the USSR: a double-edged sword given the history of relations between the CCP and the CPSU. His justification for attacking Liu Shaoqi's seniority was that it had been the Red Army (not the urban underground where Liu had operated) which had brought the CCP victory, and he attempted to recruit former rural revolutionaries to his conspiracy. Gao himself had been a graduate of the Xian Military Academy where Deng had been assigned in 1927 and had established a rural soviet in north Shaanxi which had eventually been journey's end for the Long March.

Gao's views met with some support from among others Lin Biao and Peng Dehuai, both veteran army commanders and now the party leaders of the Central-South and North-west China Regions respectively. However, it foundered when he approached Deng Xiaoping and Chen Yun. Both apparently independently brought matters out into the open at a meeting of the CCP Political Bureau in December 1953. They were concerned above all about the threat to party unity and Gao's flagrant disregard for party rules. There can be little doubt that Gao and Rao had genuinely conspired – as Deng was later to report to the National Party Conference called on the affair in March 1955 – to operate outside the established norms. Amongst other things they had promised promotion and high office to potential recruits.

The 8th Congress of the CCP

The collapse of the conspiracy led to a renewed emphasis on party unity and an exercise in damage limitation. Lin Biao and Peng Dehuai were not, unlike Gao and Rao, disgraced. Lin Biao and Deng were appointed to the CCP Political Bureau and, in addition, Deng became Director of the CCP's Organization Department, Secretary General to the CCP Central Committee, and Vice-Chairman of the National Defence Council. Peng Dehuai, who had been Commander of the Chinese People's

General Secretary of the CCP

Volunteers (the PLA by another name) in the Korean War, became Minister of National Defence. Though Deng's motivation appears to have been the maintenance of unity and the CCP's organizational strength, it seems likely that Mao drew a different conclusion about his personal loyalty.

Khrushchev, who visited Beijing later in 1954, had an interesting recollection of this relationship. He did not take to Mao, not least because the Chairman never had anything good to say about any of his colleagues in the Chinese leadership – 'Mao never recognized his comrades as his equals. He treated the people around him like pieces of furniture, useful for the time being but expendable. When in his opinion, a piece of furniture – or a comrade – became worn out and lost its usefulness, he would just throw it away and replace it ... The only one of his comrades whom Mao seemed to approve of was Teng Hsiao-p'ing [Deng Xiaoping]. I remember Mao pointing out Deng to me and saying, "See that little man there? He's highly intelligent and has a great future ahead of him."'[3]

Deng's promotions put him at the very heart of the CCP's organizational affairs and these were to be his major concern for the remainder of the decade. The other members of the Central Committee Secretariat appointed at this time were Liu Lantao, Song Renqiong, Tan Zhenlin and Yang Shangkun. Its composition was clearly designed to emphasize CCP unity, for these men together with Deng, represented the various organizational and political strands within the party. Liu Lantao had even been a former associate of Gao Gang's in the North Shaanxi Soviet. Though their paths had crossed several times since 1933, Yang Shangkun had been one of the '28 Bolsheviks' who had been actively involved in the attack on Deng in that year. However, it is a measure of Deng's networking that he had extremely good political ties to the majority of his Secretariat. Song Renqiong had been a subordinate in the 129th Division of the 8th Route Army; Tan Zhenlin had been accused together with Deng in the attack on the 'Luo Ming line'; and Liu Lantao was a protégé of Bo Yibo, a close associate of Deng's from Taihang.

The work of the Secretariat for the next two years was largely organizational, and it was a very different and more political Secretariat which was approved at the 8th CCP Congress in September 1956, when Deng was elected General Secretary of the CCP (as opposed to Secretary-General to the Central Committee). Deng had been given responsibility for the revision of the CCP Constitution and this was one of the many major changes he introduced. As he explained in his speech to the Congress, the party and its needs had changed considerably since the last congress in 1945. It had achieved national power and grown from just over a million members to about 11 million; it had previously been almost exclusively rural-based, now a disproportionate number of its members lived and worked in towns and cities. It had turned from the goals of achieving power to those of national development. To meet the changed political environment Deng proposed a complete overhaul of the CCP's organization, all of which was incorporated into the new party constitution.

Interestingly, many of Deng's proposals not only presaged the political reform programme he would initiate during the early 1980s, they also continued the principles and practices he had developed during the early 1940s in the Taihang region. One example was the need for party leadership to be strengthened by structures that clearly separated the functions and organization of the CCP and the government. Necessarily during guerrilla war the CCP's involvement in other activities was its strength. However, during the early 1950s CCP leaders frequently criticized the party's tendency to step in and run everything as dysfunctional: government units would wait on party interference and the CCP became overloaded. Deng had outlined solutions to these problems in 1941, as implemented in Taihang, in a speech to a meeting of the CCP's North China Bureau. It was later published as an article in the CCP journal *Party Life* under the title 'The Party and the Anti-Japanese Democratic Government'.[4]

However, Deng was not simply concerned with administrative matters and he dwelt at considerable length on party procedures and norms. He emphasized the CCP's traditions after 1935 as a guide to action particularly with respect to its maintenance of popular support and internal unity. This was the essential context for one of the most dramatic and misunderstood changes to the constitution. The 1945 CCP Constitution had explicitly recognized that Marxism–Leninism–Mao Zedong Thought was the party's ideology. However, Mao Zedong Thought was written out of its 1956 version.

Sources originating during the Cultural Revolution, particularly those written and distributed by the various Red Guard groups, are highly critical of Deng's action in removing the reference to Mao Zedong Thought. They regard it as *prima facie* evidence of Deng's opposition to Mao's developmental programme and his subservience to the Soviet Union. Deng had recently returned from Moscow (in April) where he had attended the 20th Congress of the CPSU and heard Khrushchev's denunciation of the cult of personality. Western commentators, for example Chang and Bonavia, have dated Deng's break with Mao from this date for similar reasons.[5]

However, Deng, like Mao and most of the CCP leadership after the early 1940s, was fiercely nationalistic. Indeed nationalism was at the heart of the concept of Mao Zedong Thought – the codification by Mao of Marxism–Leninism as applied to Chinese conditions – which Deng had propagandized so effectively throughout the 1940s. Though he did indeed criticize the cult of personality in his speech to the 8th Congress, he emphasized that unlike the CPSU the CCP had always regarded people and parties as fallible and so had never gone in for such practices. Moreover, his major concern at this time and indeed for a number of years after was with party discipline and its impact on unity. He was worried in this particular case that the status of Mao Zedong Thought was leading to a growing personalization of China's politics, and not just on Mao's side, which in turn was posing a threat to party leadership. Though he disagreed with many of Mao's ideas for China's future, he still at this time believed disagreement was possible, legitimate and desirable as long as party unity was not threatened. Deng's attitude to Mao Zedong Thought both before and after 1956 was that it certainly should be propagandized. He was simply opposed to its identification with Mao.

Deng dwelt at some length on the correct procedures for inner party debate, the requirements of collective leadership and the importance of democratic centralism. Open debate within the CCP was necessary if correct solutions were to be found to problems. In those debates individuals should be free to articulate their views. Minority views should be respected even when wrong and intra-party struggle should not lead to 'a policy of excessively harsh struggle and wanton punishment' (the so-called 'ruthless struggle' and 'merciless blows' which Deng himself had experienced in 1933). On the other hand, mistakes should not be treated by over-tolerance or over-indulgence. However, once a decision had been taken then every party member was duty-bound to carry it out. Criticism and collective leadership were necessary supports for intra-party debate. Without criticism, individuals, including leaders, could not improve their work-style and ideas. Without collective leadership politics would become personalized. Party rules were to apply impartially, there should be no 'deification of the

General Secretary of the CCP

individual' and individual leaders should not abuse their positions in dealing with either their subordinates or each other.

With the exception of Gao Gang and Rao Shushi, Deng did not name names, but his comments were nonetheless pointed, as for example when he said, 'Some responsible comrades are still prone to exercise exclusive personal control'; 'Love for the leader is essentially an expression of love for the interests of the Party, the class and the people, and not the deification of an individual'; and 'Even now not a few responsible comrades ... do not encourage and support criticism from below ... [they] use the shameful method of making personal attacks and carrying out reprisals against their critics.'[6]

Necessarily, those remarks could be interpreted as being directed at Mao. The Chairman had started to flaunt the CCP's organizational norms, notably in the summer of 1955 when he launched the 'High Tide of Agricultural Co-operativization' by appealing to provincial leaders once a central decision he did not like had been taken. He had also tried to force the leadership's hand on the pace of development in early 1956 without a proper debate. However, the behaviour which characterized Mao in his later years and which is foreshadowed in Deng's speech had not yet fully emerged. Equally, at this time others were also guilty of not observing party norms, and they too were the target of Deng's criticisms. Gao Gang's conspiracy had been built on more than two individuals and had badly shaken party unity. Nonetheless, Peng Dehuai (previously implicated with Gao Gang) from early 1956 on had started a more personalized campaign against Mao which culminated in his dismissal and the prolongation of the Great Leap Forward in mid-1959.

Deng Xiaoping

Rectification

One extremely important aspect of Deng Xiaoping's speech to the 8th CCP Congress, which came to dominate politics for the next year, was the question of party rectification. On this point there is considerable evidence that he was at odds with Mao on both the interpretation of the need for a party rectification movement and the kind of rectification that should occur. In this he was not alone, for Mao's views were not immediately shared by many in the leadership, including Liu Shaoqi and Peng Zhen (the Mayor of Beijing.)

To some extent the spectre hanging over the party debate on rectification was the challenge to communism in the USSR and Eastern Europe during 1956. The CCP delegation to the 20th Congress of the CPSU had left Moscow perturbed at Khrushchev's apparent belief that there would be a peaceful transition to socialism within the capitalist world, not least since that view undermined the basis of the support, both military and economic, they hoped to receive from the USSR. The CCP had also been concerned at the impact of liberalization in Hungary and Poland, and the threat to party rule.

Deng in his speech to the 8th CCP Congress, and later, argued that the problems of Eastern Europe could be avoided and the future of socialism in China ensured if three conditions were met: democracy within the party, party leadership and a good working relationship between the people and the party. He was generally optimistic about the CCP's achievements and prospects, arguing that class struggle was fundamentally over in China: 'The working class has become the leading class of the state; the peasantry has changed from individual farming to co-operative farming; and the bourgeoisie as a class is on its way to extinction.'

However, Deng was characteristically hard-hitting about the CCP's mistakes and he criticized what he described as a 'drift away from reality and from the masses'. Party leadership meant listening to people as well as telling them what to do – the tried and tested principles of the 'mass line' as practised before 1949 – yet since 1949 he felt that cadres had tended to rest on their laurels. Moreover, the expansion of the CCP since 1945 meant that the quality of political education was necessarily diluted.

Deng's solution to the problems of the CCP's workstyle, inner-party democracy and its relationship to the population was to launch a rectification campaign within the CCP and to establish structures for popular supervision of CCP activities. Criticism and self-criticism within the CCP would, as in the past, 'maintain Party solidarity and unity on the basis of Marxism–Leninism, [and] help comrades overcome their shortcomings and correct mistakes'. Supervision from outside the CCP would come largely through worker's congresses, people's congresses [local councils] and from the non-communist parties. Once again, Deng reached back to his Taihang experiences for inspiration.[7]

Mao's view of rectification was radically different and tied to his vision of a developmental model based almost totally on mass mobilization. Politics not economics was to be the key to future success and the solution to China's problems. In particular, he appears to have believed during 1956 and the first half of 1957 that development depended on politicizing the intellectuals and professional groups in society – of whom he was almost obsessively suspicious for much of his life – not least to create a close working relationship with the CCP. Unlike Deng, he believed that class struggle was far from over. In a famous speech in February 1957, 'On the correct handling of contradictions among the people', he outlined the nature of antagonisms that would remain even after the establishment of socialism. Some of these antagonisms would have to be dealt with forcefully, but others, the majority, required education, propaganda and mobilization to be resolved. Criticism and self-criticism needed to be extended to the whole of society otherwise the revolution would simply become bureaucratized. This wider notion of 'extended democracy' was still being explicitly denounced by Deng in early April 1957 in a report to party cadres in Xi'an, 'The Communist Party Must Accept Supervision'. Here he attributed the blame for what he described as the 'disturbances' in Eastern Europe on 'extended democracy'.[8]

Not for the last time, at the end of April 1957, Deng and others in the leadership including Peng Zhen but excluding Liu, allowed themselves to be bullied into agreeing with Mao on the grounds that party unity must be maintained at all costs. It was a bad precedent. There followed five weeks of almost unfettered criticism of the CCP in the 'Hundred Flowers Movement' of May and June and the leadership was quickly forced to call a halt. Far greater than the threat to party unity was the threat to party rule. An 'Anti-Rightist Campaign' was launched against all those who had spoken out as they had been encouraged to do. A large proportion of those who had criticized the CCP and who were later attacked were indeed intellectuals and the professional classes. As in the Cultural Revolution they were characterized as 'counter-revolutionaries' and punished severely. The long-term damage to their participation in China's development was considerable. For example, it virtually closed down the activities of the legal profession for more than twenty years.

After the campaign had ended, Deng reported on its results to the 3rd plenum of the 8th Central Committee in September 1957.[9] Unlike his pronouncements before April, his comments on the need for rectification (though not of course the form it would take) were more in accord with Mao's views on the subject. He now regarded intellectuals with some suspicion, held out the prospect of a bourgeois revival and condemned the emergence of capitalist tendencies (largely free markets) amongst the peasantry.

Of all Deng's speeches this was the one which departs the most from his Taihang vision. It has clearly proved problematical for Deng, particularly during the 1980s. Even after the Beijing Massacre, when Deng might be assumed to be prepared to take a harder line against intellectuals once again, he appears reluctant to recognize the 'Report on the Rectification Campaign' of September 1957 as his own. It is not included in the volume of his writings published in August 1989 as a political primer in the wake of the disturbances of May and June, and dealing with the years 1938–1965.

However, even in this report Deng continued to urge caution and gradualism. He emphasized that the vast majority of most social groups, including the intellectuals, were still prepared to support the CCP. Rectification and inner party democracy as he had outlined them in September 1956 were still necessary, and he stressed the need to find economic solutions to political and social problems.

The Great Leap Forward

Undoubtedly Deng's later reluctance to acknowledge the 1957 'Report on the Rectification Campaign', quite apart from its rhetoric and content, is that the 3rd plenum of the 8th Central Committee where it was delivered was the occasion on which the leadership effectively agreed to the strategy of the Great Leap Forward. The experience of the 'Hundred Flowers' was clearly a major shock for the leaders of the CCP. Within the leadership it severely dented Mao's reputation and lent force to Deng's arguments for collective leadership. It demonstrated both the need for sustained party rectification and that prolonged periods of disunity within the leadership had considerable costs. The dispute between Liu Shaoqi and Mao over rectification continued for the best part of the whole year after the 8th CCP Congress, right through the 'Hundred Flowers' of May and June 1957, and its recriminatory aftermath – despite repeated attempts by Deng during June and July to bridge the gap between them in the interests of party unity. Ironically, it also made eventual adoption of Mao's mobilization-based model of development more likely. Chen Yun's strategy for development, which had been the basis of the 2nd Five Year Plan drafted at the 8th CCP Congress had assumed the creation and encouragement of a technocratic elite. This was one reason that the intellectuals had been courted since the beginning of 1956 and encouraged to 'supervise' the CCP in May and June 1957. Now, however, their political loyalty was in doubt.

In the autumn of 1957 the CCP leadership seemed obsessed by party unity. This obsession was to last for over a year and lead to the launching of the Great Leap Forward during 1958. It was helped by Mao's announcement to his close colleagues, though not yet in public, that he would be stepping down from his position as Head of State in 1959 and replaced by Liu Shaoqi, in order to retreat to the second line of politics. Throughout most of that year, the leadership stayed united with only Zhou Enlai and Chen Yun opposing the strategy, though in effect they and the central planning bureaucracy were shunted aside from September 1957 to mid-1959.

The strategy of the Great Leap Forward called for the substitution of capital in investment by labour; the substitution of technology and economics by politics; and the substitution of expertise and skilled labour by enthusiasm. It reflected Mao's belief in the benefits to be derived from economies of scale – as summed up in his slogan of 'more, faster, better and more economical' – with no consideration of diminishing marginal utility. Its most enduring symbols were the backyard steel furnaces, which produced considerable amounts of largely useless pig iron; and the people's communes, the new and extremely large rural collectives combining economic, political and social functions for over 80 per cent of China's population. The results during 1958 appeared spectacular, as output figures reported record levels, no doubt because the State Statistical Bureau had also been taken over by enthusiasts. By November the people's communes were being hailed not simply as a successful experiment in rural living, but also as the 'sprouts of communism' – the final goal of classless society – much to the consternation of the CPSU.

However, the northern winter of 1958–9 saw many of the leaders of the CCP set out on inspection tours of the provinces to see the achievements of the Great Leap Forward for themselves. The experience was clearly a cruel shock for those, such as Deng and Peng Dehuai, who had harboured any doubts about the strategy or the man. Peng's inspection tour of his native Hunan, after he had been to Gansu, and followed by visits to Jiangxi, Anhui and Hebei, are probably the most famous because they led to his confrontation with Mao at the Lushan conference of the CCP later in 1959. However, it was by no means a unique experience. Peng found the peasants starving and local party cadres complaining in private about the excesses of the Great Leap.

Deng for his part visited several provinces, including Guizhou where on a celebratory return visit to Zunyi in January 1959 he found conditions to be unbelievably wretched given the advances of the early 1950s. There was a serious shortage of food, not least because earlier in the enthusiasm of the Great Leap, the reported record high production figures for grain had led to the peasants being directed by local cadres to 'eat until your bellies are full' and little had been kept back for seed or future supply. Deng suggested that one way to alleviate this problem was to establish communal mess halls in the people's communes, rather than everyone attempting to fend for themselves. Local leaders accepted the idea, which they appeared not to have thought of before, with some enthusiasm.[10] It was not only a practical solution to their problem but it also met the emphasis on collectivism inherent in Mao's vision and the current political rhetoric.

By February and March of 1959, Deng like many of the other more pragmatic members of the leadership was urging considerable caution. For example, at one meeting of the CCP Secretariat to discuss the importance of including productive labour in educational curricula – a favourite initiative of Mao's – he argued that while there were obvious benefits, such developments should not go too far or too fast lest they have an adverse effect on the quality of education. At another, held to discuss the people's communes, he suggested that they were perhaps not such an unqualified success, as they were continuing to have problems in production and management.

However, Peng Dehuai was less temperate than Deng, and bolstered by a personal grievance against Mao that he had been nursing for several years he started to canvass opposition to both the great Leap Forward and Mao more widely. Years later, Ye Jianying, one of the more important post-Mao leaders of the PLA was to claim that originally Deng, Liu Shaoqi, Zhou Enlai and himself all sympathized with Peng Dehuai's position. On the other hand they did not promise him support.

Unlike Mao, Peng was not a particularly skilful political manipulator, and he seems to have gone for a simple policy of surprise and confrontation at the annual summer work conference of the CCP leadership held during July 1959 in Lushan. Though he had gathered some support and written an ingeniously barbed 'Letter of Opinion' to Mao *qua* Chairman of the CCP, he had not confined his criticisms to the strategy of the Great Leap Forward but extended them to blame Mao for the excesses of the past year. In particular he accused Mao of 'leftist' errors and 'petty-bourgeois fanaticism': almost identical wording to the criticisms made by Mao's enemies during the late 1920s and early 1930s, and not epithets that Mao was likely to accept readily.

Mao counter-attacked brilliantly, not least using his position as Chairman of the CCP to control the agenda of the Lushan conference. His speech in answer to Peng's attack was measured, obscured the real issues, characterized Peng as a 'right opportunist' seeking power, and gave him no right of reply (or defence.) He also bullied, reminding his colleagues of their collective past and offering them a clear choice. Since Peng was also Minister of Defence he warned 'If the Chinese People's Liberation Army should follow Peng Dehuai, I will go to fight guerrilla war.'

Had one or two other participants spoken out in Peng's defence or to attack the Great Leap Forward, the outcome might have been different. However, Mao was not the only one taken by surprise. It seems even Peng's supporters before Lushan had not known that he was going to write a letter to Mao. In the event Mao's escalation of the conflict carried the day. The designation of Peng Dehuai and his supporters as 'right opportunists' meant that opposition to the Great Leap was temporarily stilled. Once again Mao had managed to rally the leadership to his support on the grounds of restoring party unity.

Although Deng attended the formal plenum of the Central Committee in August when Peng and his associates were denounced as an 'Anti-Party Clique' he had not attended the month-long central work conference which had preceded it and where confrontation had occurred. (Another notable absentee was Chen Yun.) There is an element of mystery here. Later during the

Cultural Revolution he was to write in his 'Confession' that he had not gone to the work conference because of trouble with his leg and had written excusing himself at the time. It sounds like a political illness, but Deng had indeed broken his leg playing table-tennis sometime before Lushan, though when is not clear. MacFarquhar suggests he broke it right at the beginning of the Lushan work conference, thus necessitating his withdrawal.[11] On balance it seems reasonable to assume that there was no political motive to his absence, but that there had been complications with his leg for some time. Certainly that would appear consistent with the photographic evidence. Neither he nor anyone else had known that a crisis of the kind that occurred was coming at the Lushan conference, and it is conceivable that he took the opportunity of the Central Committee's summer break to seek medical treatment. From December 1958 until April 1961 he was usually photographed carrying a walking stick, though that was not his normal practice either before or after.

If that inference is correct, then it may well be that Deng's visit to Moscow in late 1960 was as much in order to obtain medical treatment as to deal with Sino–Soviet relations. At this time the CCP's top leadership were taking it in turns to visit the USSR. Deng had visited in 1956 and 1957, and was not entrusted with prime responsibility in the handling of relations with the CPSU until later. Throughout the 1950s it had been the practice for Chinese leaders to seek medical treatment in the USSR.

Deng's contemporary attitude to the events at the Lushan work conference are not recorded, but it is unlikely to have been one of joy. Peng had to some extent personalized politics himself and infringed what Deng, at least, would have regarded as the norms of inner-party discipline through his clumsy attempt at conspiracy during the first half of 1959. In that context, as in the past, Mao could certainly rely on Deng for support. On the other hand, it was clear that after Lushan those norms were never going to be applied to Mao again and that the conduct of Chinese politics had changed, perhaps irrevocably. Although the Great Leap Forward was wound down in 1960 after a short burst of renewed enthusiasm and Mao withdrew to the 'second line' of politics, Deng must have been well aware by the end of the 1950s that the Chairman was too mercurial for retirement.

On the 'Capitalist Road', 1960–6   3

The period from the end of the Great Leap Forward to the start of the Cultural Revolution is probably the most obscured since the establishment of the PRC. One reason for this is that with the failure of the Great Leap the Chinese authorities imposed tighter restrictions on information of all kinds, but particularly the printed media, leaving the country. Another is that China was becoming increasingly isolated internationally. Relations with the West had been excessively low-key since the establishment of the PRC, and in the middle of 1960 Soviet advisers and technicians were withdrawn.

Partly as a result the history of these years tends to be shaped disproportionately by subsequent events in the Cultural Revolution. Then the Red Guards and those supporting Chairman Mao characterized almost all CCP leaders, but particularly Liu Shaoqi and Deng Xiaoping, as having shunted Mao aside and thereby followed the 'Capitalist Road' throughout the first half of the 1960s. Moreover, most sources of information on that period were published during the Cultural Revolution, notably by Red Guard groups competing to be loyal Maoists by denigrating 'capitalist roaders', and consequently reinforcing that perspective as well as being notoriously unreliable.

Deng certainly did come into repeated conflict with Mao and by the early 1960s they must have known they no longer shared a common vision of China's future. However, they both probably believed either that they could continue to work together, as indeed they did very successfully in foreign affairs, or that they could convince the other and the rest of the leadership to their own way of thinking. As between Mao and other leaders at this time, conflict and co-operation could and did co-exist. That is the essential context in which Deng was associated with policies and initiatives later criticized by Mao and his supporters.

The differences of opinion between Mao and Deng were more real than most, but never highly personalized. Deng was for example never criticized by name in the official media during the Cultural Revolution, but simply referred to as 'The number 2 person in authority taking the capitalist road', after Liu Shaoqi, the 'Number 1'. On the other hand, this was an important period in Deng's political development away from Mao. Changing relationships within the CCP leadership saw Deng move closer to those who would eventually be responsible with him for launching the reform era in 1978. Many of the policies discussed and implemented during the early 1960s – as with the Taihang experience, which Deng clearly drew on for some of his ideas – were to prove the basis for those at the heart of later reform.

Despite the rhetoric of the Cultural Revolution, Deng's closest working relationship at this time appears not to have been with Liu Shaoqi, to whom he had never been particularly close, nor Zhou Enlai, whom he looked up to as (in his own words of 1980) an 'elder brother' rather than a co-equal, but with Peng Zhen. Peng was the pre-Cultural Revolution Mayor of Beijing, and its first major victim. Throughout the early 1960s, they worked together to establish a new policy agenda.

Reconstruction

1960 was a truly appalling year in China. The leadership became entangled in the massive failure of the Great Leap Forward, and obsessed by the widening rift with the USSR. Agricultural output fell to about three quarters of its 1958 level. There was widespread drought and famine, and during 1959 to 1961 China's population actually fell by 13.5 million. Looking back from the 1980s, Deng was to regard the period immediately after the Lushan plenum as 'the most difficult of times,' both because of the state of the economy and relations within the leadership.[1]

The disastrous economic aftermath of the Great Leap Forward during the early 1960s would be hard to overstate. Agricultural output continued to decline and food was in short supply. Industry, which relied on agriculture for either its raw materials or capital, also went into decline. Light industry fell by 10 per cent in 1960 over the (reported) figures for the previous year, 22 per cent in 1961 and 8 per cent in 1962. Heavy industry was even harder hit, dropping by 47 per cent in 1961 over 1960 and 22 per cent in 1962 over 1961. Even contemporary newspapers, particularly at the local level, bear the scars. CCP leaders are referred to in headlines by their personal name, rather than their family name, to instil a feeling of solidarity under crisis. However, the quality of newsprint declined so much that very often the newspapers are impossible to read: thin blotting paper soaked in runny ink.

The immediate task for the CCP leadership in the wake of such massive failure had to be economic reconstruction. Emergency meetings in the second half of 1960

On the 'Capitalist Road'

brought the Great Leap Forward to an end and adopted a series of measures effectively targeted at restoring production by any measures possible in the immediate term. The economy was to be 'readjusted,' gradualism was to replace speed and agriculture was to be regarded as the key economic sector. In most cases this led to the reorganization of people's communes so that they now became reasonably manageable units. However, in some places it appears there was even complete decollectivization and individual farming was restored.

On the other hand, the leadership could not agree on what to do next; or, of equal importance, what had gone wrong and why. The CCP held a series of meetings during 1961 to discuss these matters and from the first Mao's attitude was that though there had been mistakes, the party should view the whole experience as a learning process. Liu Shaoqi, Deng and Peng Zhen and many others were as determined that nothing like the Great Leap should ever happen again so that the country should be restored to a sound economic base as quickly as possible. The potential for conflict was great.

Deng's first clash with Mao came in March 1961 at the CCP's Canton Work Conference. The conference had been called to discuss rural policy, particularly with respect to people's communes. Deng and Peng Zhen had carried out an on-the-spot investigation of the situation in a number of communes outside Beijing. They came to the conference armed with data and arguments. In particular, Deng argues that the communes had been established too quickly and without adequate preparation, discussion or investigation of specific circumstances. Mao apparently was offended by the materials Deng and Peng had prepared and discounted their conclusions on the grounds that 'without investigation, there is no right to speak.' He was obviously not impressed with their efforts to date. A year later Deng was to rise to that verbal challenge.

In the meantime the CCP had agreed, in line with Mao's *obiter dicta* to prepare a series of reports on different aspects of government work. Several committees were established, each under the leadership of a major CCP figure and with a remit to draft a policy paper. For example, Mao was given responsibility for communes, Bo Yibo for industry, Li Xiannian for finance, Zhou Yang and Lu Dingyi for culture, and Peng Zhen for education. The whole process was organized by Deng through the Secretariat, which established another three broad co-ordinating committees – one each for economics, culture, and political and legal work, chaired by respectively Chen Yun, Peng Zhen and Deng himself.

Despite Mao's participation in this planning process, he was effectively outnumbered by those who had long opposed his ideas on economic development. Not surprisingly the resulting policy papers contained recommendations that worked completely against the strategy of the Great Leap Forward: economics not politics was emphasized as the motor of development. Self-reliance was out, importing modern technology from abroad was in. Slow capital-led investment was to replace mass mobilization. Communes were to be made smaller, with the basic accounting unit reverting to the production team – the equivalent of the small co-operatives established (for the most part) in the second half of 1955. Education was to re-emphasize quality and expertise was to be valued once again. The ideas proposed at this time were to become the intellectual foundations for the reforms of the late 1970s and early 1980s. Moreover, Bo Yibo, Li Xiannian, Zhou Yang, Lu Dingyi, Peng Zhen, Chen Yun and Deng were all to play a leading role in the later reform era.

It may not have been general practice at the time but it appears that Deng and Peng Zhen established a 'think tank' of intellectuals and officials to assist them. Later in the 1980s such organizations were to be more formally organized and to play a significant political role. The group took the name of the building in which it met in Beijing's western suburbs – the Changguanlou – and through a review of all central documents for the period of the Great Leap and a series of more detailed investigations prepared reports for the two CCP leaders on a whole range of issues. They concluded that the mistakes of the recent past were a direct result of policies based on mobilization rather than planning.

Mobilization and the 'mass line' were key issues for Deng, as they had been throughout the 1950s and indeed earlier. He clearly felt that Mao had done violence to the concept of the 'mass line' by defining it only in terms of mass political campaigns. During 1961 and 1962 in particular he reflected on a number of occasions on the nature of the 'mass line', arguing presumably against Mao in the main, that there is more than one technique of mass mobilization and that mass campaigns may often be counter-productive. As he had stressed in his speech at the 8th CCP Congress, the 'mass line' entailed more sophisticated techniques, and indeed if a close relationship between party and people were to be maintained then these too must be employed, not least so that campaign weariness did not result.

Deng pursued this theme in both of his speeches to the Central Work Conference of January and February 1962. This meeting of some 7,000 party officials had been convened to come to a judgement on the Great Leap Forward and to decide on a plan for future action. He once again stressed the importance of party discipline, democracy within the CCP and party leadership. In particular, he argued strongly that those, as for example Peng Dehuai, who had been attacked as 'rightists' during the Great Leap Forward should have their cases re-examined and, where appropriate, they should be rehabilitated.

Deng also took the opportunity, as did Liu Shaoqi, to remind Mao of the value of being pragmatic. Mindful of

Mao's comments a year earlier about the importance of investigation he quoted the Chairman back at himself. In Yan'an, as Deng pointed out, Mao had urged the CCP to 'seek truth from facts'. It was an injunction that was to play an important political role in launching the reform era in 1978, but in the interim was largely ignored.

Unfortunately, the Central Work Conference was stalemated. Much was said about the need for criticism and self-criticism – for example, Mao apparently confirmed that he had made a formal self-criticism in the middle of the previous year and Deng presented a self-criticism of the CCP Secretariat – but there remained a basic split within the leadership. On the one hand there were those, like Deng, who believed the Great Leap Forward had been an economic disaster which should not be repeated, with future policies based on economic solutions. On the other, there were those supporting Mao who blamed the failures of the past on extraneous factors (the weather, the withdrawal of Soviet assistance) and inadequate politicization. In their view future success would come through a party rectification campaign and mass political education. These were to be the issues that would dominate the political agenda for the next four years and lead directly to the Cultural Revolution.

Rectification and 'class struggle'

The failure of the Central Work Conference of February 1962 to unite the leadership was exacerbated soon afterwards by the discovery that the economic crisis was worse even than the most pessimistic had predicted. The government faced a massive budgetary deficit and inflation. Deng's response, for one, was straightforward. He argued that production was the first priority and that, 'As long as we can bring about a rapid restoration, it doesn't matter how we do it,' or in the words of a speech to the

On the 'Capitalist Road'

Communist Youth League in July 1962 for which he is probably most famous, 'It does not matter whether a cat is black or white, so long as it catches mice.'[2] Deng's speech to the League was certainly no accident. He had previously taken no particular interest in youth work. On the other hand, the League's Secretary was Hu Yaobang, one of Deng's protégés since the 1940s, who was later to become CCP General Secretary himself during the 1980s.

Deng's speech directly confronted the problems of mobilizational politics, which – exactly as he had in his February 1943 speech to party cadres in Taihang – he criticized as leading too easily to over-zealous enthusiasm and 'leftist' excess. He cited examples from both industry and agriculture but saved his most trenchant criticisms for the people's communes and collectivization. Both, he said, had come about too quickly without adequate preparation, at a cost to economic production which could not be sustained. He discussed various solutions, including the redivision of collectivized landholdings, but appears not to have advocated total decollectivization at this time, as had experiments in Anhui province which presaged the individual household responsibility system introduced in the late 1970s. Instead, Deng favoured smaller collectives with production guaranteed at fixed prices on a household basis.

Mao's reaction was radically different. In the ringing tones of his injunction to 'Never forget class struggle' – announced at the CCP's summer work conference in 1962 and accepted by the 10th plenum of the Central Committee immediately following – he launched rectification campaigns aimed at both his colleagues in the leadership, and the party's organization more generally, but especially at first in the rural areas. The Socialist Education Campaign was designed to re-orientate the CCP towards Mao's vision of China's future by stressing its revolutionary past.

As envisaged by Mao, the Socialist Education Campaign would mobilize the peasantry to supervise their local party cadres, much as he had imagined the intellectuals would 'rectify' the CCP in the urban areas during the 'Hundred Flowers' of 1957. He called for the study of past injustices and class struggle as a precursor to the establishment of Poor and Lower Middle Peasants' Associations. However, it was a campaign which met with considerable resistance not only from party cadres but also from the peasantry, who in the wake of the Great Leap Forward were somewhat disillusioned with and alienated from the CCP.

In the northern summer of 1963, Deng and Peng Zhen set out to change the course of the Socialist Education Campaign – an act which later in the Cultural Revolution was to lead to considerable criticism. They left Beijing and Mao's influence for the Southwest, Deng's bailiwick during the early 1950s and where he was still well connected, in order to research the campaign's problems and to experiment with solutions. As a result they criticized the peasants' associations as being poorly organized, and suggested instead that they be led by work-teams sent out from the cities to carry out the rectification campaign. They also suggested that the first targets in the campaign should be the middle levels of the bureaucracy rather than the most local cadres. The results were of course that the whole campaign moved away from the countryside to focus on the towns and cities where the bureaucracy was located, leaving the peasants' associations with even less to do, and effectively returned rectification to an internal party matter.

During 1963 and 1964 the struggle for control of the rectification campaign continued with Liu Shaoqi further removing it from Mao's intentions by focusing on economic corruption, rather than political revisionism, as the main target. By late 1964 Mao was reaching breaking point, and in early 1965 he attempted to regain the initia-

On the 'Capitalist Road'

tive. He re-launched the Socialist Education Campaign as one of political education throughout the CCP and for the whole population. The work teams were withdrawn and their responsibilities handed back to the peasants' associations. The target was revisionism in all its manifestations, and it was at this time that Mao first raised the possibility that the CCP had been hijacked by 'those in authority taking the capitalist road'. It is unlikely that at first he had anyone specific in mind, and simply intended the remark as a warning shot to bring his colleagues into line. Within two years it was to lead to a more direct confrontation.

Mao's concern with rectification after 1962 was, however, not confined to the Socialist Education Campaign. As he developed his critique of revisionism within the CCP during the 1960s he increasingly emphasized the need for politicization in a variety of activities, including education and culture. These were particularly crucial areas for Mao as he became almost obsessed with the importance of value change – hence the usage of the term culture in the naming of the Cultural Revolution. In Mao's view all cultural and educational activities served specific political ends, and whoever controlled their implicit values also controlled society.

Lacking support for the most part within the CCP establishment, Mao had to look elsewhere for those who would help him re-politicize China. One person he turned to was Lin Biao, the Minister of National Defence, who launched a political education campaign first within the PLA, and then later when Mao launched a 'Learn from the PLA' Movement in 1963, for the whole country. The political primer for this campaign was a selection of Mao's writings in a little red book – *Quotations from the Thought of Mao Zedong*. During the Cultural Revolution Deng was criticized for his dislike of the 'little red book'. There is no contemporary evidence, but such a view would have been consistent with Deng's previous attitudes. He had always regarded Mao Zedong Thought as a product of the CCP's collective leadership and not Mao's personal property as it had effectively become. Certainly, when offered a copy of the 'little red book' as a study guide in 1970 he rejected it unceremoniously.[3]

Another person Mao turned to for support was his wife, Jiang Qing, a former actress to whom he entrusted the task of rectifying art and literature. From 1963 on she was largely successful in re-shaping Chinese culture to Mao's world view. In her own words she 'revolutionized' and 'modernized' China's traditional art forms. Culture was to reflect class struggle and serve the politics of mobilization as defined by Mao: heroic workers, peasants and soldiers were to do battle with evil landlords, capitalists and the old society. In particular she was largely responsible for promoting the eight modern revolutionary ballets and operas, which came to dominate the Chinese performing arts from 1966 to 1976. As her rectification of Chinese culture proceeded her political importance also increased, until she became part of the CCP leadership in her own right during the Cultural Revolution. Deng, apparently was unimpressed by her efforts, and said so in public on at least one occasion too many, thereby ensuring a lifelong enemy. On the eve of the Cultural Revolution, all CCP leaders were obliged to attend the performance of these new modern revolutionary operas and ballets. A common rumour, even at the time, was that Deng had managed to avoid most, but at last could procrastinate no further. He attended but made his point by falling asleep during the performance.[4]

The Sino-Soviet split

One area where Mao and Deng appear not to have been in conflict at all during the decade before the Cultural Revolution, indeed in which they seem to have co-operated remarkably successfully, was in the handling of Sino–Soviet relations. Whatever Mao may have had to say about Deng's attitude to domestic politics, he had nothing but praise for Deng's work in this area. Deng for his part, particularly during the early 1980s when Mao's role in the politics of the PRC was being reassessed, has been at great pains to stress that Mao Zedong's policy in foreign affairs had been correct and highly successful.

An essential part of the background against which the decision to launch the Great Leap Forward had been taken and which was to play an important role in the economic crisis of the early 1960s, was China's deteriorating relationship with the USSR. The search for a 'Chinese road to socialism' in and after the mid-1950s undoubtedly resulted from the CCP's inherent nationalism, but it was also a consequence of worsening Sino–Soviet relations. Though the detail is far from clear, Deng Xiaoping appears to have played a central role in the politics of the Sino–Soviet split. Between 1956 and 1963 he visited Moscow four times for discussions and often hard-headed negotiations. During the 1960s when the polemic between the CPSU and the CCP came out into the open, Deng was the formal head of the group within the CCP Central Committee – the Anti-Revisionist Writing Group – that drafted the Chinese party's replies.[5]

The Sino–Soviet Alliance had always been somewhat uneasy, more a function of Sino–American relations than of a genuine desire for co-operation on the part of the CCP. Relations between the CCP and CPSU had been difficult since the mid-1920s. A prime aim of the early 1940s rectification campaign had been the removal of Soviet influence and the nationalization of the Chinese communist movement. Their paths to power had been radically different and had resulted in competing ideological perspectives. Under the impact of conflicting mutual expectations and developments in the wider international community, co-operation rapidly turned to rancour.

From the start both sides probably had unreasonable expectations. China sought military and economic aid to a staggering degree. For most of the 1950s it was almost totally dependent on Soviet aid. When this was suddenly withdrawn in mid-1960, as the result of growing tensions, it made a disastrous economic situation in the wake of the Great Leap Forward even worse. The cost to the USSR was high at a time, when in the aftermath of the Second World War and the establishment of communist regimes in Eastern Europe it could barely afford such support. Nonetheless, China's expectation was that the USSR would supply even more economic aid, be prepared to share its nuclear technology and come to China's assistance with military force in the event of local conflicts.

In return the CCP was not willing to meet the expectations of the CPSU for military bases and co-operation, as well as for support within the world communist movement. On the contrary, the CCP seems rather to have resented the CPSU's arrogation of seniority. Partly this was personal, for after Stalin's death Mao seems to have believed that he rather than Krushchev was the next most senior communist leader. However, there was also an institutional and historical dimension to this belief since the CCP had come to power largely without, if not actually despite, the involvement of the CPSU.

In September 1954 Khrushchev came to Beijing for the first of many negotiations during the mid-1950s between the leaders of the CCP and the CPSU. The Chinese side was led by Zhou Enlai and Deng was one of the other five negotiators. Agreement was reached across a wide range of issues including the final withdrawal of Soviet troops and economic interests in China and the granting of substantial economic aid. It was the last occasion on which solid and lasting agreement was to prove possible.

February 1956 saw a Chinese delegation under Zhu De, including Deng, attend the landmark 20th Congress of the

On the 'Capitalist Road'

CPSU, at which Khrushchev criticized the cult of personality. Despite Mao's later ascribed reaction to this event and its consequences for the 8th CCP Congress when Mao Zedong Thought was written out of the party constitution, it was probably less shocking to the CCP delegation than Khrushchev's acceptance of peaceful coexistence between capitalism and socialism for this impinged on the amount of aid China could expect from the USSR, it was still possible at this stage that the USSR would have provided China with more assistance, including the nuclear technology it requested. When Mao Zedong accompanied by Deng, attended the 40th Anniversary celebrations for the Russian revolution in 1957, agreement was in fact reached to that effect, although the promise was never fulfilled.

However, in 1958 the Sino–Soviet alliance started to run into problems from which it never recovered. The CCP's insistence on a nuclear capacity was coming into increasing conflict with Khrushchev's attempts at détente and his global political strategy. The launch of the Great Leap Forward represented a significant ideological challenge to the USSR's claim to be furthest along the road to communism. Personal relations between Khrushchev and Mao were deteriorating and the CCP was becoming involved in European communist politics against Moscow.

By 1960 the Sino–Soviet split had become irreversible. CCP delegates at various meetings of international communists attacked the CPSU, and the two parties started publishing scarcely veiled critiques of each other's rapidly solidifying positions. Following the Bucharest Conference of the Romanian Workers' Party in June 1960, at which Peng Zhen and Khrushchev had a stand-up slanging match, Soviet aid to China was totally withdrawn. Under Liu Shaoqi's nominal leadership, a Chinese delegation including Deng attended two meetings in Moscow designed to heal the rifts in world communism. Both saw a series of heated exchanges between Khrushchev and Deng, which but for the intervention of Ho Chi Minh, who personally brought the two together, would have ended with no agreed communiqué. In the event the compromise was little more than a vague commitment to unity and to meet again.

The final act precipitating an open rift, which had so far been averted, came in 1963. From 1960 until that date, various communist parties, but particularly the North Vietnamese, had tried to bring the CCP and the CPSU to the negotiating table. In July 1963 Deng headed a small delegation, which included Peng Zhen, to Moscow. The failure to shore up Sino–Soviet relations was greeted as a victory over revisionism by the CCP leadership who turned out in force to welcome Deng back from Moscow. Thereafter the dispute went public through a series of highly confrontational open letters between the CCP and the CPSU. As already indicated, Deng was responsible on the Chinese side for the group that drafted the CCP's letters.

The Cultural Revolution

It is not clear when, if ever, Mao took a decision to launch an attack of the scale of the Cultural Revolution on the CCP leadership. Deng at the time of Mao's reassessment in 1980–81 on one occasion reflected that Mao had in fact never intended to attack veteran cadres to such an extent. A theory that once Mao had set the conflict in motion it developed a dynamic of its own is easy enough to sustain. The CCP leadership was not only split ideologically by 1966, it was also split organizationally. Though the details are hard to trace it seems that both those who supported Mao and those who opposed his world view were using different parts of the central political system to set their own agenda and to attempt to implement their own policies. In the ensuing

On the 'Capitalist Road'

chaos, and under the pressure of the Red Guards Mao had called into existence, politics became wildly unpredictable.

Peng Zhen was to be the first major victim of the Cultural Revolution. Apparently under consideration by Mao as his potential successor during the 1960s, Peng had been given the task in 1965 of extending rectification and politicization into the educational sector. A Cultural Revolution Group was established under Peng's leadership, but when it reported in February 1966 it ran into opposition and thus led to Peng's removal, along with several supporters including the current President of the PRC, Yang Shangkun. A new Cultural Revolution Group was established in May which included Deng. However, it also included a majority of those who, unlike Deng, supported Mao in his belief in the power of mobilizational politics.

By August and the 11th plenum of the CCP Central Committee, Deng found himself along with Liu Shaoqi repeatedly under attack. At a meeting of the Cultural Revolution Group he was characterized by Chen Boda as 'the spearhead of the erroneous line', though Mao is reported to have given both him and Liu another chance to 'correct their mistakes'. However, by October it was clear that Deng would not escape punishment. He was required to present a formal self-criticism – detailing how he had opposed Mao Zedong and Mao Zedong Thought – to a Central Work Conference on 23 October, and several years of incarceration were to follow.

In the Cultural Revolution, Deng, along with all the other CCP leaders who had been purged, were reviled as a 'revisionist' clique who had wormed their way into the CCP in order to subvert the Chinese revolution. Though he was only ever referred to officially as the 'Number 2 person in authority taking the capitalist road' his 'crimes' were dissected at length by wall posters and in Red Guard publications. According to some of these accounts, he continued to protest his innocence stubbornly throughout, as he had done in 1933.[6]

Deng Xiaoping

Mao's criticisms of Deng, also disseminated unofficially during the Cultural Revolution, dwelt at length on Deng's personal conduct as well as his espousal of 'revisionist' policy preferences. One of Mao's major compiaints was that Deng had sidelined him in various ways after the Great Leap Forward. Deng and Liu, said Mao, 'had treated me like I was their dead parent at a funeral', forgetting perhaps that it had been at his suggestion not theirs that he had retired to the second line of governance. In addition, according to Mao, at meetings Deng had used to position himself as far away as possible so that he did not have to hear what the Chairman was saying – although Deng is profoundly deaf in his right ear. Whether that was true or not, Deng was to pay dearly for his opposition to Mao.

Cartoon published in a Red Guard publication during the Cultural Revolution depicting the Revisionist Gang enjoying a sumptuous banquet. Deng is portrayed as the fifth figure seated on the left. Moving round the table from right to left the figures depicted are Li Weihan, Bo Yibo, Peng Zhen, Liu Shaoqi, Wang Guangmei, Tao Zhu (standing), Deng, He Long, Luo Ruiqing, and Yang Shangkun.[7]

The pendulum years, 1969-78

4

Almost nothing is known about what happened to Deng between 1966 and 1969. It appears he was struggled against for about a year and then kept in solitary confinement for another two. However, the decade after Deng was released from imprisonment in 1969 was extremely eventful. In the course of that decade he twice spent periods in internal exile, only to return on each occasion to the centre of the political stage and the highest levels of party leadership. Unlike the 1950s when a spirit of unity pervaded the CCP, the 1970s was a period of intense party factionalism. The CCP leadership was increasingly divided over the results of the Cultural Revolution; the efficacy, or otherwise, of Mao's mobilizational approach to development; and the question of the succession to Mao. In this uncertain political environment Deng was helped by his past relationships not only with Mao Zedong and Zhou Enlai, but also (and of greater importance in the long run) by those who had been his subordinates during the Sino–Japanese War and the War of Liberation.

Jiangxi days

During 1967 and 1968 the Cultural Revolution severely disrupted the work of the CCP and the state administration. Even the direct intervention of the PLA in civilian politics from the beginning of 1967 was not an immediate check on the political chaos. The PLA was no more united in political terms than the CCP, and though under Lin Biao's direction (and in support of Mao) it was directed to 'restore order' it often ended up becoming embroiled in local factionalism.

Order was eventually restored by early 1969, shortly before the CCP's 9th Congress was convened, but it was a very new political order. In particular, by 1969 civilian politics was heavily dominated by PLA officers. Of course, the relationship between the CCP and the PLA had always been close, not least because of the communist path to power before 1949. Thus, most of those who held positions of leadership within the CCP between 1949 and 1985 – essentially the first revolutionary generation of the PRC's leadership – had some army background in addition to their CCP experience. However, the extent to which actively serving PLA officers had come to dominate the CCP by 1969 was a new development. Almost half of the new CCP Central Committee elected in 1969 were concurrently in the PLA. If not exactly a South American definition of a military junta, this was still an inordinately high involvement of military personnel in government.

The restoration of administrative order and the worsening Sino–Soviet relations across China's northern borders led in late 1969 to the decision to disperse the CCP's purged leaders being held in Beijing to other parts of the country. Despite its presentation in the Red Guard press, Deng's case had always been differentiated from that of Liu Shaoqi and other pre-Cultural Revolution leaders, not least by Mao Zedong who is rumoured to have said something to that effect at the 9th CCP Congress. Certainly, Zhou Enlai seems to have gone considerably out of his way to assure a suitable reception for Deng when he was sent out of Beijing in October 1969.

Deng was sent to Xinjian County in Jiangxi province, where for three and a quarter years he was theoretically under house arrest in a former infantry academy whilst working part-time in a nearby tractor repair plant. With him went his wife, Zhuo Lin, and his step-mother Xia Bogen. Of the three Deng, at the age of 65, was undoubtedly the fittest and part of the mythology of this episode in Deng's life which was promoted during the 1980s is the picture of Deng cleaning, cutting wood and breaking up coal.[1]

Life was undoubtedly very hard for Deng and his family, particularly before the end of 1971. However, a remarkable feature of the time they spent in Xinjian is the extent to which local conditions were adapted by Deng's 'minders' to make life more comfortable within the parameters established by Beijing. Partly this may have been the result of Zhou Enlai's influence, or the genuine respect of the local people for Deng. It was almost certainly helped by the fact that the party secretary of the factory where Deng worked had served under him during the Sino–Japanese War.

When Deng and his immediate family had arrived in Xinjian it had been under strict guard and instructions that limited their activities. Yet within a short while, a special path had been laid for Deng and his wife to cover the two kilometres from where they lived to the factory where they worked so that they would not have to walk on the public highway; it was whimsically dubbed the 'Deng Xiaoping trail' by the locals alluding to the then Vietnam War. Deng was allowed to keep chickens and he and Zhou Lin started a vegetable garden. Deng was even instructed in how to make his own wine and spirits by a local woman.

Deng Xiaoping

Eventually, he was even allowed to have his children move in with the rest of the family in Jiangxi. For Deng Pufang, the eldest son, this was rather important. During the Cultural Revolution Deng Pufang, who had been a physics student, had been expelled from the CCP and either thrown from an upper-floor window according to one report, or pushed down a flight of stairs according to another, by Red Guards because his father was a 'capitalist roader'. The attack had left him paralysed, confined to a wheelchair, and living for a while in a welfare centre. In 1972 he was allowed to travel to Beijing, with his sister, to receive proper medical treatment. However, by then it was too late for remedial action. By the time Deng returned to Beijing in 1973 ten members of the family had been reunited in Jiangxi.

In September 1971, Lin Biao died, probably but by no means certainly in an aircrash over Mongolia after having unsuccessfully tried to hang on to power within the CCP. The news reached Xinjian and Deng Xiaoping in November. It appears that within a very short time the attitude of Deng's jailers changed dramatically for the better. Local party officials up to the provincial level started coming to call. In early 1972 Mao Zedong attended the memorial meeting for Chen Yi – a former foreign minister and military leader who had served with Deng during the Huai–Hai Campaign – and is reported to have spoken favourably of Deng to Chen's children. In August 1972 Deng wrote to Mao Zedong and the CCP Central Committee through Wang Dongxing asking to be allowed to return to work. In Beijing it appears that Wang Zhen and Wang Jiaxiang both lobbied Mao on Deng's behalf and at the beginning of March 1973 the CCP Central Committee passed a resolution which recalled Deng from Jiangxi. His first post-Cultural Revolution public engagement was at an official banquet for Prince Sihanouk, of Cambodia, when he passed almost unnoticed by the Western press corps.

The Pendulum Years

The 'Four Modernizations'

Several explanations have been provided for Deng's rehabilitation in 1973. The generational structure of the CCP leadership before the Cultural Revolution meant that it would be difficult to replace the large number of those who had been purged during 1967 to 1968 with enough competent cadres within a reasonable period of time. Significantly, at the same time that Deng was rehabilitated other leaders who had also been in disgrace or criticized during the Cultural Revolution were rehabilitated or brought back into active service, including Chen Yun and Tan Zhenlin. Lin Biao's death and the subsequent removal of his supporters from the CCP and the PLA may have left Mao feeling that the new leadership was not balanced the way he would prefer between the more radical forces of Jiang Qing and the more moderating influences of Zhou Enlai. Zhou Enlai, for his part, may have felt that Deng would be an ally against radicalism within the leadership.

All these explanations probably contain an element of truth. In addition, it seems reasonable to assume that there was considerable goodwill extended towards Deng generally within the leadership. Although Deng and his civilian associates had been purged during the Cultural Revolution, one irony of those events was that they had resulted in a disproportionately large number of Deng's former military subordinates – from Taihang, the 129th Division of the 8th Route Army and the 2nd Field Army of the PLA which grew out of it – being promoted to leadership posts in both the CCP and the PLA. With the removal from the leadership of Lin Biao and his supporters – who had had a different experience during the Sino–Japanese War, and were of another Field Army – that disproportion was magnified still further.

Of course, loyalty ties of this kind are not an exclusive or particularly precise predictor of political or factional activity. Deng's former subordinates in Taihang, for example, included Li Xuefeng, Xie Fuzhi, and Ji Dengkui, all of whom became famous as Cultural Revolutionary radicals to a greater or lesser extent within the CCP Political Bureau. However, by the beginning of 1973 when the Political Bureau had only 16 members, six – Liu Bocheng, Chen Xilian, Xu Shiyou, Su Zhenhua, Ji Dengkui and Li Desheng – had served with or under Deng in Taihang during the Sino–Japanese War. A seventh, Chen Yonggui, the peasant leader from Dazhai, had also been there at the same time but there is no evidence of personal contact with Deng.

Deng's appointment as Vice-Premier brought him into immediate conflict with the more radical elements of the CCP leadership. Jiang Qing and her associates, Zhang Chunqiao, Yao Wenyuan and Wang Hongwen – later to be characterized as the 'Gang of Four' – derived the legitimacy of their position in the leadership from their close relationship to Mao and their emergence during the Cultural Revolution. As a result throughout the 1970s until their arrest in October 1976 they campaigned strongly to protect what they regarded as the 'new-born experiences' of the Cultural Revolution: for example, the replacement of party committees and people's governments by revolutionary committees; the encouragement of 'open door schooling' (learning on the job) rather than any technical training; and positive discrimination in social, educational and economic activities for those classified as soldiers, workers or peasants. Deng not only had a wider and more independent legitimacy in the history of the CCP, he also remained opposed to the politics of mobilization.

On the eve of the 10th CCP Congress, shortly after Deng's recall, the 'Gang of Four', undoubtedly concerned by the prospect of Deng and Zhou Enlai working together again, launched oblique attacks on them both disguised as criticism of the now-departed Lin Biao. This opposition intensified when Deng was reappointed to the CCP's Political Bureau and Military Affairs Commission at the end of 1973 (he had been elected to the 10th Central Committee along with a number of other prominent victims of the Cultural Revolution in August) and was to continue for the next three years. In the context of the coming succession to Mao, for the latter was increasingly ill and frail for the remainder of his life after the 10th CCP Congress, Deng despite his own advanced years was seen as the main rival. Thus, when Deng led a delegation to the United Nations in 1974, where he spoke on Mao's 'Theory of the three worlds', he was criticized, together with Zhou, by Jiang Qing on his return for their handling of foreign affairs.

At the end of 1974 relations between Deng and the 'Gang of Four' worsened. Zhou Enlai was seriously ill and in hospital. Deng replaced Zhou as the person responsible for overseeing the routine work of the CCP and the government, and was appointed 1st Vice-Premier, Vice-Chairman of the CCP, and Chief of staff of the PLA. From this position he was able to do much to set what he saw as a necessary new policy agenda. Although his activities were necessarily constrained, he was able to have a few of his pre-Cultural Revolution supporters, notably Hu Yaobang and Hu Qiaomu, brought back into active service. Under Deng's co-ordination and with the assistance of other leaders as well as the support of the State Planning Commission, as in the early 1960s a series of policy reports were commissioned.

Deng's new policy agenda was referred to as the 'Four Modernizations' and took its cue from Zhou Enlai's 'Report on the work of the government' presented to the National People's Congress in January 1975. Here Zhou referred to the very general idea he had articulated, with Mao's support, in 1964 that China should ensure the 'comprehensive modernization of agriculture, industry, national defence, and science and technology before the end of the century'. Deng organized a series of meetings and conferences during 1975 at which the goals and methods for achieving the 'Four Modernizations' were discussed. At least three documents were drafted: 'On the general programme of work for the whole party and the whole nation', 'Some problems in accelerating industrial development' and 'On some problems in the field of science and technology'.[2]

Deng himself spoke out on the need to modernize the PLA, railway transport, and the iron and steel industry. The essence of his vision was the almost complete negation of Mao's politics of mobilization and the Cultural Revolution. Deng and his supporters emphasized the importance of classroom education, and of providing workers and peasants with material incentives to encourage them to produce more rather than relying largely on ideological exhortation. It was argued that China should abandon its policy of economic self-reliance and expand its foreign trade. In particular, it was suggested that the PRC should export raw materials such as coal and oil, as well as manufactured chemical products (mainly coal by-products) in order to import 'high-grade, high-precision, advanced technology and equipment so as to speed up the technical transformation of our industries and to raise the productivity of labour'. The PLA was criticized, and not just from outside its ranks, for being 'over-expanded ... inefficient ... and not combat-worthy', which given the role of the PLA in the CCP's tradition, and especially in Mao's vision, was sailing very close to the wind indeed. Even closer perhaps was Deng's stated desire to see quality and gradualism replace quantity and speed in economic production.[3]

The Pendulum Years

The Tiananmen Incident, 1976

Deng's critique of the Cultural Revolution was by no means confined to economic development. Once again, he returned to his constant preoccupations with party leadership and party discipline, which he described as having been threatened and destroyed by the Cultural Revolution. Under cover of attacking Lin Biao, he effectively criticized the dependence on the power of Mao Zedong's words which the Cultural Revolution had created. His argument was essentially that Mao Zedong Thought could not be reduced to only a few quotations. This was simply the 'fragmentation of Mao Zedong Thought' which resulted in the CCP becoming 'divorced from reality and the masses'.[4] In his view Mao Zedong Thought had to be constantly tested in practice, though he did not yet, as he was to do in 1978, refer back to Mao's comment of the need to 'seek truth from facts'.

As at the 8th CCP Congress in 1956 Deng advocated a rectification of the CCP according to the principles originally articulated by the party during the early 1940s. Indeed, he made specific reference to the party's heritage from the Sino–Japanese War on a number of occasions. According to Deng, the CCP had more recently omitted 'to integrate theory with practice, maintain close ties with the masses, and practise self-criticism'. The results were that the CCP had become characterized by factionalism, and there was a shortage of suitable party officials, particularly at the basic level.

These comments were clearly not intended to appeal to Deng's opponents within the CCP leadership. However, as 1975 progressed he went further and called for a re-examination of the cases of those, like himself, who had been purged at the start of the Cultural Revolution. This was a direct threat to the position of those who owed their position in the leadership to those events and it eventually led to his dismissal in 1976.

Deng Xiaoping

Throughout 1975 the radical elements within the CCP leadership had tried to keep Deng in check. In March and April, Yao Wenyuan and Zhang Chunqiao launched an attack on Deng's policies by claiming that they would lead to the restoration of capitalism in China. In particular, Deng's proposal that there should be an incentive scheme to improve production was characterized as the thin edge of the wedge. Though unnamed, Deng and Zhou were characterized as revisionists and 'rightists' who opposed Mao Zedong's vision.

Later in the year Deng was more specifically targeted in a trial by allegory that became front-page news. The lack of open and institutionalized politics, particularly during the Mao-dominated era of Chinese politics, meant that contemporary political debate was often presented as reinterpretations of history or classical literature. In this case, the focus was on the famous *Water Margin* story and one of its heroes, Song Jiang. Song Jiang is an immensely popular figure in Chinese culture, China's equivalent in many ways of Robin Hood, an outlaw who eventually takes service with the Emperor. The debate which started during late 1975 was about whether Song Jiang should be viewed more critically for having capitulated to the establishment. For Song Jiang the Chinese public were to read Deng Xiaoping, under attack for capitulating to capitalism.

For most of 1975 it appears that Deng was able to call on Mao's approval for his actions. Mao was ill and dying at this time, and it is more than possible that he may not have had a clear grasp of what was going on in the wider politics around him. However, as Deng's proposals to reverse the Cultural Revolution gathered pace, so did Mao's concerns, particularly when Deng argued that the cases of those criticized at that time should be re-examined. At a meeting of the CCP Political Bureau in early November, Deng was deprived of all his responsibilities except in foreign affairs – where he had taken responsibility for negotiations on the establishment of diplomatic relations with the USA and led a delegation to France – and a political campaign was launched against the 'Right deviation of reversing correct verdicts'.

Deng's position as the successor to both Mao and Zhou was taken by Hua Guofeng, a provincial party secretary who had risen to national prominence during the Cultural Revolution. In January 1976, when Zhou Enlai died, he was appointed Acting Premier and placed in charge of the CCP Central Committee's daily routine. That the move to shunt Deng aside met with considerable confusion and resistance was to become clear very shortly. Nonetheless, radical attacks on Deng, his policies, and the memory of Zhou Enlai, continued. In late March, the Shanghai newspaper *Wenhui Bao* carried a lead article which criticized 'that capitalist-roader within the party who had wanted to reinstate in power the capitalist-roader who had been overthrown and is unrepentant to this day.'

Reaction to the *Wenhui Bao* article in Nanjing, provincial capital of Jiangsu, was intense. There were mass demonstrations against the dishonouring of Zhou Enlai's memory, and for Deng and the 'Four Modernizations.' A few days later, as news of the Nanjing Incident (as it became known) spread to Beijing, the same was to happen there. 4 April 1976 was *Qing Ming*, or the Festival of Sweeping the Graves, when Chinese traditionally pay homage to the dead. It provided an excellent opportunity to organize demonstrations in memory of Zhou Enlai, and by extension in support of Deng Xiaoping, and against the largely unpopular 'Gang of Four'. Crowds flocked to Tiananmen Square in the middle of Beijing on 4 April with floral wreaths to Zhou Enlai, and poems making political points about Zhou and Jiang Qing, all of which were placed round the Revolutionary Martyrs Memorial in the centre of the square.

On the evening of 4 April, the area was cleared of the

wreaths and poems by local security forces. Popular reaction on 5 April was extremely hostile, and it was not long before the fast-gathering crowd turned violent. Its targets were those associated with the 'Gang of Four' and the repressive power of the state. Thus, at least one student from Qinghua University in Beijing, where the Cultural Revolution radicals had established a 'think tank', was set up and hung from a lamp-post. A police station on the south of the square was set on fire. Towards evening, there were several ugly scenes and the

A Hong Kong view of the call for Deng's reinstatement during 1976 and 1977[5]

crowd was only dispersed by the use of force. Public security forces were called in by the Mayor of Beijing, Wu De, with the assistance of the Minister of Public Security (as well as acting Premier) Hua Guofeng, and the commander of the guard unit attached to the CCP Political Bureau, Wang Dongxing, all of whom were members of the Political Bureau.

Meeting on 6 and 7 April 1976, the CCP Political Bureau denounced the demonstrations as a 'counter-revolutionary incident' for which Deng was somehow responsible; dismissed Deng from all his posts in the CCP and government; and appointed Hua Guofeng as First Vice-Chairman of the CCP and Premier of the State Council. Carefully stage-managed demonstrations followed in which Deng's supporters from the central economic planning institutions in particular were forced to march round Tiananmen Square denouncing him. For several months Deng was characterized in the media in almost identical terms to those used during the Cultural Revolution as 'the bourgeoisie within the communist party', and the three major reports prepared in 1975 were denounced as 'the three poisonous weeds'. At the same time, other 'veteran cadres' who had long been associated with Deng, notably his two erstwhile bridge partners, Hu Yaobang and Wan Li, were forced out of office as they had been in the Cultural Revolution.

The 3rd plenum of the 11th CCP Central Committee

Though the official media may have treated Deng as it had during the Cultural Revolution, Deng was not otherwise abused as he had been at that time. Under the protection of Xu Shiyou, who commanded the Canton Military Region, and who was a member of the CCP Political Bureau and a former subordinate from the Sino–Japanese War, he went south to Canton. Chinese politics were clearly extremely unstable at that time and almost anything could happen. On 9 September 1976 Mao Zedong died, and the question of the succession finally had to be settled. Despite their aspirations, the 'Gang of Four' had during the 1970s successfully alienated both their own social constituency and any other potential support within the party leadership. The result was that their relationship with Mao Zedong had become almost their only base of support. Within a month of his death, the CCP had arrested them and elected Hua Guofeng Chairman of the CCP.

In exile in Canton Deng had reportedly outlined three conditions which he insisted should be met before he was prepared to be rehabilitated once again. He insisted that the Tiananmen Incident of April, and his role in it, should be reconsidered; that he should be reinstated in the positions he held before the end of 1975; and that his reinstatement should be approved by both a National People's Congress and a CCP Congress. Though he was to reappear in public before all three conditions were met in full, by the end of 1978 they had all been fulfilled.

The delay, and indeed the source of most of the problems generally at this time, was that Chinese politics could not be readily freed from the influence of ten years of Cultural Revolution. One immediate problem was that Deng's return, which was generally expected, was necessarily related to Hua Guofeng's future, since the latter had only become First Vice-Chairman of the CCP because of Deng's dismissal at the end of 1975. Another was that the CCP leadership had to decide how much of the Cultural Revolution it was going to reject.

Deng apparently wrote to Hua Guofeng shortly after the latter's confirmation as Chairman of the CCP, requesting permission to go back to work. Chen Yun, Li Xiannian, Ye Jianying, the Minister of National Defence, and Wang Zhen, who had lobbied Mao on Deng's behalf in 1972 and was now Vice-Premier, were loud in their

The Pendulum Years

calls for his return. Hua was prepared to stall on the holding of a CCP Central Committee meeting where these pressures would undoubtedly lead to a resolution for Deng's return, in order to try and marshal support.

An attempt to build a 'personality cult' around Hua was launched through the official media. Considerable publicity was afforded Hua's quasi-official appointment by Mao as the latter's successor on 30 April when Mao was reported to have told Hua, 'With you in charge, I'm at ease.' In January 1977, building on this relationship with Mao, Hua argued at a CCP Political Bureau meeting that 'We must resolutely uphold whatever policy decisions Chairman Mao made and unswervingly carry out whatever Chairman Mao instructed' – a statement that later became known as the 'two whatevers'. Hua's position was supported by several other members of the leadership, who though they had not been followers of the 'Gang of Four' nonetheless owed their positions to promotion during the Cultural Revolution.

However, the tide was running too fast against Hua not least because after Mao's death and the arrest of the 'Gang of Four' those who had been the victims of the Cultural Revolution were being rehabilitated in increasing numbers. In addition, Hua needed to call a CCP Central Committee meeting in order to legitimize the arrest of the 'Gang of Four' and to confirm his own position. In March, a Central Work Conference agreed to Deng's reinstatement to all the positions he had held at the end of 1975, but left the time of his recall to Hua Guofeng. After an exchange of correspondence between Deng and Hua, the stage was set for a meeting of the CCP Central Committee and both Deng's return to active politics and Hua's confirmation as Chairman of the CCP. It was to be a hollow victory for Hua.

Almost immediately, at the 11th CCP Congress which was held in August 1977, Deng attacked, if obliquely at first, Hua's 'two whatevers'. Whereas Hua's speech to the conference brought this Cultural Revolution to an end by promising that 'in line with Mao Zedong Thought' it would not be the only one and there would be more in the future, Deng by stressing the need to revive the CCP's traditions and work-style promised the opposite.[6] Indeed, by the end of the year Deng had already started to implement the plans that had been on the drawing board since at least 1975, with the introduction of a scheme for the modernization of the PLA.

In March 1978 the second of Deng's conditions for his recall was fulfilled when the 5th National People's Congress met in Beijing. By that time a 'Counter Cultural Revolution' was already well under way. Following Mao's death there had been a dramatic turnover in the leadership as great as that which had occurred at the height of the Cultural Revolution. However, this time it was the victims of 1967–68 who returned to power, and unsurprisingly their support went to Deng and those campaigning for a full rejection of the Cultural Revolution.

Deng's position during 1978 was so secure that he was able to visit a number of countries in East and Southeast Asia; to finalize arrangements for the establishment of diplomatic relations with the USA (which he had been responsible for negotiating in 1974–5); and to announce new policies on intellectuals and education which effectively reversed those of the Cultural Revolution; at the same time he manoeuvred against Hua. With Hu Yaobang's assistance a seminal article was published in May which provided the ideological basis of the changes to come. Entitled 'Practice is the sole criterion of truth', it took its ideological cue from Mao's Yan'an injunction (which had resurfaced in 1962) to 'seek truth from facts'. Essentially it argued that the importance of Mao Zedong Thought was in the perspectives and general principles it provided, not in the letter of its quotations. This was a view Deng had held for some time, and used most recently in his conflicts with the 'Gang of Four.'

In 1977 it had been necessary for Deng to admit that he had committed mistakes. By the end of 1978 the criticisms of CCP leaders were increasingly focusing on the 'mistakes' of those who had supported the 'two whatevers'. The immediate climax came at the landmark 3rd plenum of the 11th Central Committee and the Central Work Conference which preceded it. Together they lasted for most of November and December, at a time when a 'Democracy Movement' (no doubt inspired by events at the Central Work Conference) was developing on Beijing's streets, when it was announced that diplomatic relations were to be established with the USA, and when border tensions with Vietnam were increasing.

The Central Work Conference must have been one of the most remarkable in the history of the CCP and has certainly been presented that way since, as it signalled the final rejection of the Cultural Revolution and the start of the reform era. It decided to make economic modernization the most important priority; to introduce political, administrative and legal reforms designed to support economic modernization; to reverse the verdicts on a number of key pre-Cultural Revolution leaders of the CCP who had not yet been rehabilitated, of whom two were Deng's close associates Bo Yibo and Peng Zhen, as well as Tao Zhu and Peng Dehuai; to restore party democracy; to decollectivize agriculture; and after a preliminary assessment, to carry out a more thoroughgoing reassessment of Mao Zedong and the Cultural Revolution some time in the future. It also met the third of Deng's conditions for his recall and declared that the Tiananmen Incident far from being 'counter-revolutionary' was 'a completely revolutionary event'.

Though all the outcomes of the 3rd plenum were not immediately apparent at the time, in effect Hua Guofeng had lost the battle to maintain his leadership of the CCP, and Deng, whatever formal position he held, became the real leader. The policies on economic modernization he had supported in the early 1960s and again in the mid-1970s could now be implemented, and the team which had co-operated in their design was now together again in command of the CCP and the economy. The policies on party leadership and party discipline, which Deng had tirelessly advocated since the 1950s, could now be given their first real chance since the 1940s to be put into practice. For Deng the 3rd plenum was undoubtedly a great success, but the real challenge of putting his vision into practice still lay ahead.

Reform and reaction, 1979-89   5

The period from the 3rd plenum of December 1978 to Deng Xiaoping's formal retirement in November 1989 may be divided into two. Before September 1985, and the special National Conference of the CCP, economic and political reforms were put into effect, on the whole with considerable success. However, after that date, when incidentally Deng retreated from the daily routine of politics and government, the reform agenda began to lose its momentum in the face of several major economic and political problems. Political stability, based on the party democracy Deng had long advocated, characterized the early 1980s. Although factionalism as in the Cultural Revolution did not re-emerge during the late 1980s, nonetheless political differences within the leadership became more acute, especially during 1988-89.

With some justification Deng is regarded as the architect of reform. However, he led a collective leadership and his contribution in many areas of the reform programme was to create the conditions for others to act rather than being directly responsible himself. Thus, though he did not ignore economic reform, he left its precise direction to others, particularly those who had come together to draft the proposals for China's economic recovery and development during the early 1980s – Chen Yun, Bo Yibo, Peng Zhen and Li Xiannian – as well as a new generation of front-rank leaders including Zhao Ziyang and Wan Li.

Deng for his part concentrated on two major policy areas: political reform and foreign affairs. An early concern was to ensure the final rejection of the Cultural Revolution, necessarily related to Deng's longer-term attempts to establish party democracy and a more open – though still limited – political system. That last goal proved particularly elusive not least because of its inherent ambiguity. The tension between a more open political system and the principle of party leadership was a recurrent theme throughout the 1980s, even before attempts at compromise broke down in May 1989.

In foreign affairs, Deng met with greater success in gradually mapping out for China a genuinely independent foreign policy, while embracing at the same time international interdependence. The 'Open door' policy has had considerable impact on the Chinese economy, though possibly not as much as Western businessmen would like. Increasing détente between the CCP and CPSU during the decade led to the restoration of party-to-party relationships, and Gorbachev's visit, under the most difficult of circumstances, to Beijing in May 1989. In 1984, tough negotiations with the UK led to an agreement for Hong Kong to pass to PRC jurisdiction in 1997.

'Problems inherited from history'

The success of Deng Xiaoping and his supporters at the 3rd plenum left three major problems requiring immediate attention. The CCP had committed itself to both economic and political reform but had not detailed precisely what either meant. Indeed, as Deng was later to acknowledge (in 1987 when talking to Korosec, of the Communist League of Yugoslavia) the popular reaction to reform after the 3rd plenum took many leaders by surprise. In addition, there were what Deng described as the 'problems inherited from history'.[1] The CCP had to decide what to do with the 'Gang of Four' now under arrest; and how, as it had indicated at the 3rd plenum, it was going to reassess the Cultural Revolution, Mao Zedong's role in Chinese politics and the nature of Mao Zedong Thought. Necessarily, such questions were also related to the future of Hua Guofeng and his supporters. Though they were at least partially responsible for the arrest of the 'Gang of Four', they had nonetheless entered the leadership as a direct result of the Cultural Revolution.

During 1976 to 1978 the Chinese economy had overheated, in ways which were to become cyclically familiar during the 1980s. A period of rapid growth was associated with excessive capital construction, the use of foreign investment to non-productive ends, severe economic imbalances and the spectre of runaway inflation. At the beginning of 1979 with the economic planners of the 1960s back in control a series of meetings were held which decided that the current economic development plan would be revised and a period of 'readjustment, reform, consolidation and improvement' introduced for the next three years.

Nonetheless, even at this early stage the general direction to be set for the economic reforms was clearly visible. A key principle in both Chen Yun's and Deng's thinking was that the over-bureaucratized state machinery was simply not up to running in a flexible way the production process in a modernizing economy. Instead, they proposed that production units should be given more autonomy in management, not only from CCP interference – which during the Cultural Revolution had meant that political work often replaced production as the main activity – but also from government. With the exception of a few sizeable enterprises in strategic industries, local and central government was to be drawn back from what had been one of its main activities.

Support for Deng in experimenting with these economic ideas came from Wan Li and Zhao Ziyang, both of whom had served under Deng in the border region centred on Taihang during the 1940s. Wan was also a long-time bridge partner of Deng's from before the Cultural Revolution, who had been removed from office as one of Deng's supporters in both the Cultural Revolution and 1976. In the late 1970s he was the leading party secretary in Anhui province where he oversaw the de-collectivization of agriculture and the introduction of the responsibility system. It was an experience which was to become a model for the rest of China. Essentially, this meant that each peasant household would farm its own land and undertake responsibility to produce a given output, on a contractual basis, which the state guaranteed to purchase. As had been Deng's policy in the early 1940s, any surplus produced could be disposed of by the peasant household as it chose. In the late 1970s Zhao Ziyang was the leading party secretary in Sichuan province where he not only implemented such rural reforms but was also responsible for the introduction of similar ideas – often referred to as the 'Sichuan experiment' – into industrial enterprises. Interestingly, in both cases this was not the first time such economic reforms had been suggested. Sichuan had proposed similar ideas in 1956 and Anhui in the early 1960s.

A further feature of the new economic order was the Special Economic Zones. At the major Central Work Conference called to discuss economic reforms in April 1979, Deng proposed that these should be established in southern China's Guangdong province, adjacent to Hong Kong. The intention was not simply that they should be a device for integrating Hong Kong into the PRC, but rather areas of derestricted economic activity where foreign technology and investment could be introduced into China. In the process it was undoubtedly hoped that any potentially harmful influences which might be imported along with foreign technology might be restricted in their impact by being limited to the Special Economic Zones.

Despite these changes away from the centralized, planned economy, Deng's emphasis in 1979, and indeed throughout the 1980s, did not abandon his commitment to socialism. In economics, Deng, though considerably less forcefully than Chen Yun, has always regarded the public sector as the leading sector in the economy. In politics he had gone much further to make it clear that he does not believe the central role of the CCP can or should be questioned at all. For Deng, democracy is a matter of making the communist party state more efficient.

The challenge to Deng's central belief in party rule was one of the first items to be of concern immediately after the 3rd plenum. Undoubtedly aware of the politics that were being acted out behind closed doors at the end of 1978 a 'Democracy movement' had come alive on the streets of Beijing and other cities. For the most part demonstrators were part of the 'loyal opposition' who thought they had approval to call for democracy, since that was indeed a key word at the 3rd plenum. There were, however, one or two challenges to the CCP's monopoly of political power. Deng's reaction was swift in defining the new 'socialist democracy'. At a forum on theoretical work at the end of March 1979 Deng outlined the 'Four basic principles' by which acceptable political behaviour could be judged: 'Keep to the socialist road ... uphold the dictatorship of the proletariat ... uphold the leadership of the Communist Party ... uphold Marxism–Leninism and Mao Zedong Thought.'[2]

The reassessment of CCP history was less easily determined, not least because it had implications for Hua

Guofeng and his supporters. It was also related to the treatment of the 'Gang of Four'. Deng's emphasis on the need for democracy and legality in order to support modernization virtually ensured they would be put on trial, if only for educational purposes. A trial would propagandize the rejection of the Cultural Revolution, and the importance of legal processes. However, the trial was delayed while the wider issues were discussed. As always, Deng wanted the CCP to make a clear distinction between Mao Zedong personally and Mao Zedong Thought as the codification of the collective wisdom of the CCP before 1949. He also wanted a clear distinction to be made between Mao Zedong Thought and Mao's actions after 1958. If these distinctions were not made, and the 'Gang of Four' rather than Mao Zedong, were held responsible for the Cultural Revolution, then Hua had a chance of maintaining his position. If, on the other hand, Mao was held responsible for the Cultural Revolution and could be said to have negated Mao Zedong Thought himself after 1958, then all his subsequent actions were suspect and Hua was out on a limb.

In the event, the Cultural Revolution was rejected according to Deng's interpretation. The 'Resolution on certain questions in the history of our party since the founding of the People's Republic of China' was drafted by a small group led by Hu Qiaomu, under the supervision of Deng and Hu Yaobang during 1980, and was circulated for discussion several times before it was finally adopted by the 6th plenum of the 11th Central Committee of the CCP in June 1981. By then Hua Guofeng and others in the leadership had bowed to the inevitable.

Deng insisted that an essential part of the rejection of the Cultural Revolution should be that its victims, like Deng himself, be fully reinstated. This process continued in 1979 with a whole stream of Deng's former close associates – including Bo Yibo and Peng Zhen – and several others such as Yang Shangkun being restored to membership of the Central Committee. At the same time Peng Zhen was reappointed (and Zhao Ziyang was appointed for the first time) to the CCP Political Bureau. In February 1980, Liu Shaoqi was posthumously rehabilitated, and four members of the Political Bureau who had supported Hua Guofeng's 'two whatevers' were removed from the leadership. However, these were not purges. In line with Deng's new emphasis on party democracy, these were demotions: neither life nor livelihood were threatened. In the middle of 1980 Zhao replaced Hua as Premier; and at the end of 1980, the trials of both the 'Gang of Four' and those 'co-conspirators' of Lin Biao's who were still alive began, with predictable results. By then Hua had offered to resign as Chairman of the CCP, to be replaced by Hu Yaobang after Deng had refused the post on grounds of age (he was by then 76, though he did become Chairman of the Central Military Commission.) Interestingly, in the spirit of the new politics, Deng offered Hua the Vice-Chairmanship of the CCP, which the latter in turn declined.

'Socialism with Chinese characteristics'

The 'Resolution on CCP history' played an important role in Deng's plans for political reform. While it criticized Hua Guofeng for 'left' errors during the two years after Mao's death and decisively rejected the Cultural Revolution for which it held Mao himself primarily responsible, it was its reinterpretation of Mao Zedong Thought and the CCP's traditions which supported Deng's vision. Mao Zedong Thought was essentially redefined in terms of those traditions – the integration of theory with practice ('seek truth from facts'), party democracy and the close relationship between party and people – and the purpose of political reform was to restore those traditions.

Though the reinterpretation of Mao Zedong Thought

was only formally accepted by the CCP in June 1981, Deng had been consistently arguing that case for some time. In particular, his speech to the CCP Political Bureau in August 1980 – 'On the reform of the system of party and state leadership' – was the most thorough statement of his views on political reform.[3] He stressed the need for the routinization of government, for the rejuvenation of the leadership, for the re-establishment of party democracy and the maintenance of party-led democracy. These became common themes in Deng's politics throughout the 1980s and indeed, have strong resonances going back to the early 1940s.

In Deng's view the routinization of government was necessary in order to encourage both economic modernization and good relations between party and people. There had to be an efficient separation of the functions of party and government, individuals had to be more restricted in their spheres of influence and an administrative order had to be created. These requirements arose from his criticism of three tendencies which had become particularly acute during the Cultural Revolution, but which had been long-term problems faced by the CCP. One was the tendency for the party to step in and replace government, which he had first addressed in the early 1940s in Taihang. According to Deng the CCP should guide not govern. If it replaced government then neither performed efficiently. Government waited on CCP interference and the latter became over-loaded. A second tendency was the over-concentration of authority, not only in the CCP's hands, but in the hands of specific individuals who had come to monopolize positions of leadership in the CCP, PLA and government, thereby personalizing politics as well as leading to inefficiency. A third and associated tendency was that within the bureaucracy, systems of responsibility and administrative regulations were frequently absent.

Deng's call for the rejuvenation of the CCP pulled no

punches, either in 1980 or later, and remarkably for the most part Deng has been prepared to accept the same advice he has handed out to others. In his speech of 1980 he pointed out that too many of the leaders of the CCP were either too old, too ill or too inexperienced to carry out the new tasks of economic modernization facing the PRC. He recommended retirement as soon as possible for those of the revolutionary generation who had been purged in the Cultural Revolution and only recently reinstated. To this end and to allow these veterans to continue to play a role in contemporary politics, Deng suggested in 1982 the temporary creation of a Central Advisory Commission as a 'second chamber' to the CCP Central Committee. In 1989 it was to play a crucial role in the unfolding political crisis. However, Deng was also concerned with the longer-term prospects of succession. He wanted to ensure that in future there should be more orderly generational change. To this end he proposed that the CCP should have a training programme in which it identified likely leaders for the future and that it abolish the system of life-long tenure for cadres.

These suggestions were all linked to Deng's vision of party discipline and the re-establishment of party democracy.[4] The personalized and dogmatic politics of the Cultural Revolution were to be replaced by a system based on collective leadership, discussion and debate. According to Deng, the CCP should accept that mistakes do inevitably happen and attempt to mitigate their consequences. Disciplinary problems should be handled within the CCP and to this end he proposed the re-establishment at the 12th CCP Congress in 1982 of a control commission, in the form of the Central Discipline and Control Commission, under Chen Yun's leadership. The rules for individual party members and for political behaviour within the CCP were set out in the 'Guiding Principles for Inner-Party Life' adopted in 1980. Of greatest importance, Deng insisted that party affairs had to be kept within the CCP and he had no time for Mao's 1950s notion of 'extended democracy'. (Indeed in 1980 he also moved to remove the guarantees of 'extended democracy' – the rights to 'speak out freely, air views fully, hold great debates, and write wall-posters' – from the constitution of the PRC.) In the same spirit, at the 12th CCP Congress, the position of CCP Chairman, created for Mao Zedong, was abolished and replaced by the post of General Secretary.

The final plank in Deng's programme of political reform was the encouragement of party-led democracy. Both sides of that imperative were central to Deng's vision. He emphasized the need to stimulate individual and group initiative within society. In particular, Deng went out of his way to re-enlist the intellectuals – the 'stinking ninth' category of counter-revolutionaries, as they had been castigated during the Cultural Revolution – to the cause of economic modernization. However, as his 1979 announcement of the 'Four basic principles' made clear, the resulting more open society could not challenge the leadership of the CCP. Deng's vision of technocratic democracy was detailed crisply in his 1987 meeting with Korosec:

> 'The greatest advantage of the socialist system [over liberal democracy] is that when the central leadership makes a decision it is promptly implemented without interference from any other quarters ... we don't have to go through a lot of repetitive discussion and consultation, with one branch of government holding up another and decisions being made but not carried out. From this point of view our system is very efficient.'[5]

The corollary of that position was Deng's emphasis on the need to combat what he described as Western or bourgeois influences. In 1982 he called for the creation of a 'socialist spiritual civilization' to support the CCP's drive for economic modernization. As he pointed out when meeting the Spanish Vice-Premier, Alfonso Guerra, in 1987, 'Some of our young people ... are not clear about what capitalism is and what socialism is. So we have to educate them about these things.'[6] On four occasions during the 1980s – in 1981, 1983, 1986 and 1989 – he took the lead in launching political campaigns against 'spiritual pollution' or 'bourgeois liberalization'. In January 1986, at a meeting of the CCP Political Bureau, he even singled out an individual Chinese writer, Zhou Erfu, for attack (and consequent expulsion from the CCP) because the latter had reportedly visited a Japanese war shrine, and had also visited a red light district when in Japan.

Deng's programme for political reform was part of his much wider vision for China's future. At the 12th CCP Congress of September 1982 he described this as the attempt to 'build socialism with Chinese characteristics'. In addition to political and economic reform, that vision rested on a more active foreign policy. Deng's 'open-door policy' was designed, within limits, to bring the PRC more into the world, and the world into the PRC in order to assist economic modernization.

One tangible sign of the 'open-door policy' has been the Special Economic Zones. Originally established in Guangdong province, another was later added in Fujian province (on the east coast) and yet another on Hainan Island (in 1988). At the start of 1984, the existence of the zones was questioned, largely because they were seen as importers of 'spiritual pollution'. However, following a visit by Deng the policy was extended to some 14 coastal cities which were granted similar economic rights to encourage foreign investment and trade.

The other side of Deng's desire for China to be part of the international economic order was a fierce nationalism and a drive for a truly independent foreign policy. As Deng said to almost every foreign visitor he met during the 1980s, but particularly those from communist Eastern Europe, no one is entitled to tell China what to do, because the conditions in every country are unique. The perspective led Deng from a near alliance with the USA at the end of the 1970s, to the establishment of better relations between the CCP and the CPSU at the end of the 1980s.

There is no suggestion that the USA had tried to dictate terms to the PRC. It is even possible that Deng, mindful of the experience of Sino–Soviet relations in the 1950s and 1960s with which he had been intimately involved, had always intended the PRC's close relations with the USA during the late 1970s to be temporary.[7] However, after his famous visit to the USA in 1979 – when among other things he appeared on television at a barbecue and wearing a ten-gallon hat – Deng acted decisively to ensure that over-dependence on either superpower was avoided. Throughout the 1980s, and not always in response to Soviet overtures, he spent considerable time and energy indicating his conditions for the restoration of CCP–CPSU relations, largely the mutual recognition of equality and independence. Perhaps with an aging politician's sense of history he seemed proud to welcome Gorbachev to Beijing in May 1989. It was a long way from his statement at the 3rd plenum of the 10th Central Committee in 1977 that 'In almost no likelihood will my generation or the generation of Comrade Hua Guofeng and Wang Dongxing or even the following generation ever re-establish close contact with the CPSU.'[8]

Deng's nationalism was also evident closer to home. It is not known to what extent Deng initiated the decision to invade Vietnam in early 1979, after conflict along the border, though it is clear he was at the meeting which took the final decision. However, Deng was closely involved in the negotiations over the future of Hong Kong and the policy of 'One country, two systems' is widely attributed to him. Under this rubric, in 1984 the PRC agreed that Hong Kong's social and political system, clearly different from that in the PRC, could continue to exist even after Hong Kong passes from British to PRC jurisdiction in 1997. The agreement on Hong Kong was, of course, a sufficient economic and political goal in itself. However, the bigger prize Deng was chasing was Taiwan.

The national party conference of 1985

The economic reform programme was spectacularly successful through to 1984, though up to that time reform had largely concentrated on rural China. By 1983 the targets of the 1981–85 Five Year Plan had been met two years early and it began to look as if the general plan of quadrupling income per capita by the year 2000 might be achieved quite easily. Rural industry was beginning to grow rapidly as a result of increased economic wealth in the countryside and the standard of living of most Chinese had improved.

Politically, the PRC had survived its longest period of stability for some considerable time. Intra-party disputes, though perhaps not meeting Deng's ideal description of such processes, had been kept within bounds and resolved without the dogmatism and violence of the Cultural Revolution. Though the Cultural Revolution's legacy in terms of factionalism took longer to disappear than was officially recognized, it was no longer an important determinant of politics. A legal system had been re-established and the system of government overhauled.

There were, however, problems ahead. Although the post-3rd plenum leadership had been extremely united in knowing what it did not want, its unity was considerably more fragile when it came to deciding how to proceed. There was general broad agreement that China needed to import foreign technology, to be part of the international economic order, to introduce market forces into the economy, to plan according to economic rather than political criteria, to regularize politics and to relax controls. However, there was also considerable disagreement on the extent to which and the means by which these goals should be achieved. For the moment, there were more immediate problems, but this disagreement created difficulties which could not in the longer term be ignored.

A more immediate set of problems came with a minor economic crisis. In October 1984 the decision was taken to extend the principles of economic reform, particularly the extent of enterprise autonomy, to the urban areas. The result, in the final quarter of 1984 was a massive inflationary boost to the economy as urban economic enterprises took advantage of their new-found freedoms. As in the recent past, Deng had left the detail of economic management to others. However, as 1985 progressed – and with it the drafting of the Seventh Five Year Plan to be introduced in 1986 – it became clearer that there was a sharp disagreement between those on whom Deng had previously depended, notably Chen Yun and Zhao Ziyang.

Deng for his part had run into problems with his attempts to reform both the PLA and the leadership of the CCP. Deng's decision to reform the PLA during the mid-1980s is politically hard to plot. During the mid-1970s the PLA had been solid in its support for Deng and the policy of modernization.

Though it had not wanted to abandon its political roles completely, it had clearly wanted advanced weaponry and to become more of a professional army. It is possible that Deng decided the PLA required reform after the disastrous results of the invasion of Vietnam in early 1979 when the PLA did not live up to its own propaganda and was forced to withdraw before it became bogged down. It is also possible that Deng decided to take the lead in reorganizing the PLA because he realized that he

Reform and Reaction

had a better chance than anyone else of carrying through a programme of reform. He had a distinguished war record and a long association with the army. He had ceased to be Chief-of-staff in 1980, but had just been appointed Chairman of the Central Military Commission. Moreover, he had used that position to ensure considerable support by promoting former subordinates, particularly from the Taihang region during the Sino–Japanese War. One example was Yang Dezhi, who had replaced him as Chief-of-staff.

Nonetheless, Deng ran into trouble with his planned reform. Ye Jianying, who had supported Deng during the troubled days of the mid-1970s was reportedly apoplectic. The essence of Deng's proposals was the attempt to bring PLA spending under control, to increase its efficiency, to rejuvenate its officer corps and generally to create a more professional army. He argued that its troop strength be reduced by about one million; that most of its veteran officers and cadres retire; that the 11 military regions be reduced to seven more related to China's geo-strategic situation; and that each of the PLA's constituent armies be reorganized, so that they no longer reflected the infantry-based requirements of the 1940s, which had remained the PLA's order of battle. In the end, Deng was successful, but only by relying almost totally on support from his former subordinates, mainly from Taihang and the 129th Division, but also from the 2nd Field Army. As a result of reorganization, by the end of 1985 of the 17 senior generals in the PLA ten were former subordinates of Deng Xiaoping. Both of the military commissions responsible for military affairs – one for the state, the other for the party – were also almost totally dominated by Deng's former associates.[9]

Deng's rejuvenation of the CCP leadership had progressed relatively smoothly after the 12th CCP Congress in 1982. However, there remained a substantial number of veteran cadres, including some who were PLA officers, resisting retirement. The rejuvenation of the leadership and discussion of economic reform were the agenda of a special National Party Conference which had been scheduled since the previous October for September 1985. In the event the Conference displayed a unity not to be repeated during the 1980s, though not without considerable conflict.

The compromise that was stitched together on the economy was inherently unstable. Whilst all speakers pledged themselves to the Seventh Five Year Plan to be introduced in 1986, they clearly disagreed on the emphases they favoured. Chen Yun, for example, issued dire warnings about the importance of market regulation remaining subordinate to planning. In particular he argued that the CCP should intervene to ensure that grain production (which had reached record levels in 1984) remained high, even though it had dropped as a result of the rural reforms which directed the peasants into cash crops and other activities. He also expressed concern that party members had lost their communist ideals. Deng could easily agree with that last point, but was more reticent on the first, affirming both that the predominance of the public sector and common prosperity were the fundamental principles in the process of economic reform.

Leadership rejuvenation was also agreed at the Conference, but at a cost. A substantial number of the more elderly members of the CCP leadership, including several veteran PLA officers such as Ye Jianying, were persuaded to stand down, and they were replaced by younger, better educated and generally more technocratically oriented leaders. The best examples are three of those who were added to the CCP Political Bureau at that time: Li Peng, Qiao Shi and Hu Qili, all of whom were university graduates then in their late 50s or early 60s. However, the veterans' resistance had only been overcome on the understanding that, as in the early 1960s, the CCP leadership was to be divided into two lines with Deng and the older remaining members of the Political Bureau withdrawing from the daily political routine to the second line. As in the early 1960s that division was to make the position of those supposed to be responsible for the CCP's routine administration largely untenable.

Tiananmen 1989

After 1985 the CCP leadership increasingly polarized around two different visions of reform. One was of a market-determined economy with a routinized and relatively open political system, though still having a ruling communist party. The other was of a planned economy, modified by market-oriented policies, with considerably less political liberalization where the CCP and the state continued to dominate the economy and society. The former more liberal attitude was characterized as emphasizing an immediate need for both economic and political reform; the latter more conservative view as stressing a more gradualist approach to economic reform, and extreme reluctance with regard to any political reform. The key issues of debate were the introduction of price reform to meet the new pressures imposed on the economy by the extension of reform to the urban sector, and the separation of party and government.

The more liberal vision of reform was promoted by Zhao Ziyang, the Premier of the State Council, and Hu Yaobang, the General Secretary of the CCP, generally at least at first with the support of Deng Xiaoping. In the mid-1980s and until late 1986 they seemed to have seized the initiative. Plans for the introduction of price reforms were discussed and drafted, and in April 1986 experiments with further political reforms and particularly the separation of party and government were started in Taiyuan. At that point relations between Deng and Hu

Yaobang appear to have gone awry. Like Mao, Deng had frequently mentioned the possibility of his retirement. Indeed, it even seems likely that Deng had wanted to retire. However, at the beginning of August 1986 he had told a Japanese guest that he was not to be allowed to do so.

In early September one of the more liberal newspapers carried an article urging Deng's retirement on two counts: it would help pull the rug from under the feet of those who argued against the abolition of the system of lifelong tenure for cadres; and it would enable a more democratic system to be established. Deng was extremely concerned by the extent to which this article and some of the political reforms being implemented were leading to suggestions of a wider political democracy. At the 6th plenum of the 12th Central Committee in late September he spoke determinedly against the possibility. However, over the next two months Hu Yaobang reportedly fanned speculation of Deng's retirement in that context. At a meeting of the CCP Secretariat in late November there was apparently an angry showdown between Hu and Deng, with the former suggesting he should replace Deng as the Chairman of the Central Military Commission and the latter declaring that Hu had forfeited Deng's trust. As a result, the meeting decided that Zhao would replace Hu as General Secretary of the CCP at the up-coming 13th CCP Congress, scheduled for October 1987.

In the event, student street demonstrations for greater democracy erupted at the end of 1986 and provided the opportunity for the opponents of all reform to demand Hu Yaobang's removal in January 1987. Zhao Ziyang became Acting General Secretary of the CCP immediately, and Wan Li became Acting Premier in his place. For the third time during the 1980s Deng sanctioned a political campaign against 'bourgeois liberalization'. Nonetheless, by the 13th CCP Congress, with Deng's influence the balance once more seemed to have swung back in favour of more liberal reform. At the Congress, Zhao's report argued that China was in the 'primary stage of socialism' when the development of productive forces had to be the CCP's priority, rather than any political concerns with socialism.

In elections to the Central Committee, which for the very first time involved an element of genuine choice, party delegates rejected a number of those most closely associated with opposition to reform. Although Deng retired formally from the CCP Political Bureau, so too did Chen Yun and Peng Zhen, the two most notable advocates of the more conservative vision of reform. On the other hand, it appears that at the Congress the new CCP leadership semi-formally recognized Deng as the 'paramount' leader.

In late 1987 and early 1988 Zhao was ready to press ahead with economic reforms, particularly of the pricing system. The introduction of market structures alongside the institutions of the command economy had led to economic difficulties not least because of price differentials between the two sectors. Zhao sought the introduction of a full market system for the determination of prices. However, his opponents highlighted the political dangers which included not only the CCP's decreased ability to direct the economy, but also their concerns about the possible effects on the CCP's natural constituencies of support should (as they feared) price reform prove inflationary.

Experiments with price reform were implemented during the first half of 1988, but in late July the CCP's leadership postponed any such initiatives indefinitely. At that time it became clear that the leadership's worst fears might be about to be realized and that China was headed for an inflationary crisis. Prices soared, goods were stockpiled and there was a run on the banks. Zhao's position and indeed that of the more liberal vision of reform became extremely exposed. At a meeting to discuss the crisis he was reported to have lost his temper with Li Peng, who had succeeded him as Premier, and threatened resignation. He need not have bothered, for the CCP Political Bureau removed him from the economic policy-making process when it met in August. The reversal owed much to Deng's change of heart. Although he had supported price reform in the first half of 1988 and indeed pushed Zhao to go further and faster, by July he indicated that he had an open mind on the subject and saw no need to stand unreservedly behind Zhao.[10]

It was the combination of inflationary crisis and frustrated democratic aspirations that made the student demonstrations, centred once again on Tiananmen Square in the middle of Beijing, so threatening to the CCP. The demonstrations started in April 1989 as memorial marches for Hu Yaobang who had died on 15 April – a martyr in the students' eyes to the democratic cause they had championed at the end of 1986 – and quickly rallied the urban workforce, largely for economic reasons, to the cause of change. Moreover, the longer the demonstrations continued without state intervention, the more people became convinced that their participation was at least officially sanctioned.

It is still too soon to determine with any hope of accuracy Deng's precise role in these and subsequent events. It is possible to take the view that Deng had, in contrast to his earlier views and practices, simply become an old man impatient with change who had given up listening. However, all the available evidence would seem to suggest that Deng simply stuck with characteristic stubbornness to his principle that party rule cannot be challenged. As early as 25 April Deng had commented adversely on the demonstrations in response to a report delivered to him by Li Peng, the Premier, and Yang Shangkun, the President. Deng had criticized the demonstrators as wanting to overthrow the CCP. He clearly

Reform and Reaction

believed, wrongly as it turned out, that they were simply a student minority who had been stirred up by an irresponsible Hu Yaobang when he was alive. Deng called for the *People's Daily* to issue a forceful editorial, to be followed if necessary by the suppression of the demonstrations by the security forces. He warned 'We must do our best to avoid bloodshed, but we should foresee that it might not be possible to completely avoid bloodshed.'[11]

The next day's *People's Daily* did indeed carry a strongly worded editorial that among other things described the demonstrations as a 'planned conspiracy to plunge the whole country into chaos'. The reaction the following day was to ensure that Tiananmen Square saw the biggest and most carefully organized anti-government demonstration in the history of the PRC. Zhao Ziyang at the time was in North Korea. When he returned to Beijing on 30 April he attempted to distance himself from Deng's hard line and made public statements which encouraged the demonstrators to believe compromise was possible.

Deng is reported to have been furious with Zhao's breach of CCP discipline. According to party reference materials, Deng made it abundantly clear that Zhao's attempts at reconciliation with the demonstrators on 3 and 4 May 'represented only his personal point of view' and not that of his position (as General Secretary) or of the CCP. A meeting of the leadership on 9 May, attended not only by members of the Political Bureau but also by former senior party leaders now 'relegated' to the Central Advisory Commission or simply retired – notable among whom were Chen Yun, Peng Zhen, Bo Yibo and Li Xiannian – discussed what to do next and, it seems likely, decided on the imposition of martial law.

However, nothing could happen immediately for on 11 May Gorbachev was scheduled to arrive in Beijing. To the outside world, the 'summit' in Beijing was not quite the media event that had been promised – attention was directed elsewhere to the events in Tiananmen Square. It is impossible to know whether Deng felt humiliated by receiving Gorbachev under such circumstances, or whether he continued in his belief that the demonstrations were the conspiracy of a small minority. There are no confirmed details (though much speculation) on Deng's behaviour from then, through the declaration of martial law in Beijing on 19 May, to the forced evacuation of Tiananmen Square on 4 June and its associated street fighting and loss of life.

On 9 June in reviewing the events surrounding what he now described as a 'counter-revolutionary rebellion' Deng was remarkably calm about what had happened. In an obvious effort to downplay the lasting significance of both demonstrations for democracy and the use of troops to suppress those demonstrations, he argued that 'This storm was bound to happen' because political work and education had been inadequate. According to Deng the strategy of reform and the 'Four basic principles' were correct but they had not been 'thoroughly implemented. They had not been used as the basic concepts to educate the people, to educate the students, and to educate all the cadres and communist party members.'

Deng went on to praise the PLA, its loyalty to the CCP and the sacrifices its members had made, including laying down their lives, in putting down the rebellion: 'they did not forget the people, the teachings of the party, or the interests of the nation ... this army retains the traditions of the old Red Army ... this army of ours is forever an army under the leadership of the party, forever the defender of the country, forever the defender of socialism, forever the defender of the public interest.'[12] It was a message repeated in all the printed and electronic media at the time. Deng, for example, was seen on television personally congratulating troops that had been involved in the suppression of the 'counter-revolutionary incident'.

Reform and Reaction

'The old man and his dog'

A Hong Kong view of Deng's reaction to the demonstrations of 1989. The dog on Deng's right has Premier Li Peng's head. The spittoon on his left is marked 'democracy'.[13]

Throughout the remainder of 1989 Deng was to be more high profile in the official media than he had been for some considerable time. He was reported meeting various visitors to China, including Kim Il-sung from North Korea who paid an 'unofficial' visit in November doubtless to discuss developments in the communist world. Three books of his writings, including one covering the years 1938–65, and a two-volume collection on literature and the arts were published in as many months. In September a new film about an episode in

Deng's life – *The Bose Uprising* – was released to considerable fanfare.

At the 5th plenum of the 13th CCP Central Committee, held in November, Deng finally announced his resignation from the Chairmanship of the Central Military Commission and his retirement from politics. On 13 November he entertained his last official visitors – a Japanese business delegation – at the Great Hall of the People of Beijing, and said, 'I will take this opportunity to bid farewell to my political life and political career.'[14] It was a grand gesture, without much real content. By the end of the month he was once again hitting the headlines when he called on Julius Nyerere of Tanzania, only this time in an unofficial capacity, during the latter's visit to China.

Comrade Deng: a preliminary assessment 6

Undoubtedly for some time to come in the public consciousness worldwide Deng will be associated with the massacre in Beijing during June 1989. The images associated with first the demonstrations, and then the use of military force in Tiananmen Square and its surroundings, were extremely powerful. The precise detail of Deng's role in the events of 1989 may remain in doubt, but not his general attitude as demonstrated by his praise for the PLA units involved. Had he died or even retired before June 1989, history's judgement would probably have been very different. However, a picture of Deng as a liberal reformer would always have been a mistake. Redefining and extending rights have never been Deng's major concerns, but rather party rule, party discipline and economic production, in that order of priority. Indeed, even his desire after 1976 to liberalize the worst excesses of the system created by Mao Zedong and the Cultural Revolution was derived from his vision of the CCP as the panacea for all China's ills.

Any assessment of Deng Xiaoping is likely to be difficult, particularly while he still lives and so close to the events of 1989. Moreover, the presentation of Deng in the

Deng Xiaoping

Chinese media remains a very potent political symbol for the leadership of the CCP, as it did throughout the 1980s. Indeed, one of the paradoxes of the reform era has been that while Deng has attempted to depersonalize politics and emphasize collective leadership, such changes have been driven to a large extent by his own personal authority. Thus the first collection of his writings to be published (the volume covering the years 1975–82) was produced to act as a primer for the rectification campaign of 1983. In that volume Deng was quite definitely portrayed as the guardian of the CCP. In other volumes and in the media generally throughout the 1980s Deng has also been portrayed as a family man, a soldier, a statesman, and a reformer. These different images provide a useful focus for preliminary assessment.

The family man

Deng has clearly revelled in his portrayal as a family man. Newspapers, magazines and books in China have shown plenty of photographs of him with his five children during the 1980s. A cynic might argue that this portrayal is largely political. Powerful politicians often like to have their photographs taken holding young children or with their families: it is supposed to soften their public image and make them seem more like the rest of the world. This may even be true in Deng's case, but if so Deng has surely gone to great lengths for the sake of an image.

It seems reasonable to assume that like most Chinese Deng has a strong emotional attachment to his family. Unlike many revolutionaries – and Mao Zedong was a notable case in point – he has managed to retain that orientation. In 1949, despite having been away from home for 29 years, when he returned to Chongqing he gathered his family back together and, except for a short break during the Cultural Revolution, he managed to look

A Preliminary Assessment

after his step-mother from then until her death. In and after 1969 when exiled to Jiangxi, he did his best to bring all the family together again, even in adversity. In the 1980s whenever he went on an inspection tour of the provinces, however distant from Beijing, he seems to have taken one of his several grandchildren along.

Apart from that, details of Deng's personality are largely unavailable. His daughter Maomao has described him as a very private man. He is 'an introvert and has few words ... He is rather philosophical on the question of personal fate ... optimistic in the face of adversity.'[1] Mao clearly recognized some of the same qualities: 'Deng is a rare and talented man. Deng has ideas. He does not assault problems head on without thought. He finds solutions. He deals with difficult problems responsibly.' However, Mao also recognized his stubbornness and the ability to know what he wanted and to go for it when he said, 'Deng's mind is round and actions are square.'[2] These were important qualities in a career which included three forced military marches and three purges.

It would seem that Deng's appearance is in itself disarming. This is not so much a function of his height – Deng is only a little over five feet tall – as his face. Photographs of Deng from the 1930s and 1940s well into the 1980s show a lively and open expression. Deng clearly does have a keen sense of fun. An enthusiastic and capable bridge player – Hu Yaobang and Wan Li were both long-term partners – he has never apparently played for money. Rather the losers have to crawl on all fours under the table. However, there is also a steely side to Deng's nature, as his actions in the political in-fighting of the early 1960s and again between 1973 and 1978 bear witness. In Mao's description, Deng was 'a needle wrapped in cotton'. On the whole, and unlike many of those with whom he worked, his relations with his colleagues normally appeared at least professionally cordial. The exception was an apparently profound

Deng Xiaoping

dislike for the radicals of the Cultural Revolution. One, Chen Boda, once complained that 'Discussing with Deng Xiaoping as equals is more difficult than putting a ladder against heaven.'[3] Deng seems to have done little to hide his animosity towards either Jiang Qing or Lin Biao.

Remarkably, his willingness to abide by the norms of intra-party democracy seems to have been extended even to those against whom he might well have been thought to have a justified grudge. Hua Guofeng had replaced him as successor to both Zhou Enlai and Mao Zedong in 1976, yet when Deng was in control again after 1978 he was prepared to reach an accommodation with Hua. In 1933 when Deng was severely criticized, imprisoned and probably tortured by the CCP, the attack had been led by Li Weihan who was aided and abetted by Yang Shangkun. Deng's wife at the time, Jin Weiying, even divorced him to marry Li Weihan. Yet Deng not only worked amicably with them both after 1949, but after they both had been purged in the Cultural Revolution he did not oppose their reinstatement in 1978. Li died in 1984 when a Vice-Chairman of the CCP's Central Advisory Commission, but Yang was promoted to be President of the PRC in 1988. Deng's relationship with Yang is even closer, for one of his daughters married Yang's son.

At the same time, Deng appears not to have forgotten his old friends and colleagues, even posthumously. One of those who bore the brunt of the attack against Mao Zedong and the 'Luo Ming line' in 1933 along with Deng was Mao Zetan, Mao Zedong's youngest brother. Left behind when the Long March retreated from Jiangxi he was immediately captured and executed by the Nationalists in 1934. Like most of Mao's family from before he married Jiang Qing, Mao Zetan was largely unremembered publicly until after the Cultural Revolution. In 1986 Deng went to Jiangxi and opened a memorial to Mao Zetan, which he had personally inscribed.

A Preliminary Assessment

The soldier

During the 1980s the CCP promoted Deng's image as a soldier. This was not based on his activities as Vice-Chairman of the National Defence Council before the Cultural Revolution, nor as Chief-of-staff of the PLA during the second half of the 1970s, nor as Chairman of the Military Affairs Committee for most of the 1980s, but rather on his war record during the years 1938 to 1949. At that time Deng had been the political commissar of first the 129th Division of the 8th Route Army, and then, after the Sino–Japanese War and during the War of Liberation against the Nationalists, the Shanxi–Hebei–Henan–Shandong Army which became the 2nd Field Army of the PLA. During the late 1980s plays, books and films appeared which dealt in particular with the 2nd Field Army's march south to the Dabie Mountains in 1947 and the Huai–Hai Campaign of 1948–9.[4]

The popularization of Deng's role as a soldier in the mid-1980s probably resulted from his and the CCP leadership's desire to reorganize the PLA and to rejuvenate its leadership. Deng was much better placed than anyone else in the leadership to bring that about and if necessary to bridge any division that might arise between the CCP and the PLA. Unlike many of those he had come into contact with between 1929, when he went to Guangxi, and the victory of 1949, Deng was not a career soldier. For example, Zhang Yunyi, who he worked with in Guangxi; Liu Bocheng; and Chen Yi, who commanded the 3rd Field Army during the Huai–Hai Campaign, were all professional soldiers rather than party cadres. Nonetheless, through his organizational and political skills, Deng managed to gain their confidence and acceptance.

The publicity afforded Deng as a soldier during the second half of 1989 was presumably also the result of contemporary politics. The message of the CCP was one of the essential unity between the CCP and PLA, as had existed in the Sino–Japanese War and the War of Liberation. It was a message directed not only at the population as a whole, but also towards the PLA some of whose soldiers were undoubtedly concerned at the use of force against unarmed civilians.

The portrayal of Deng Xiaoping as a soldier of some military skill may seem a little odd at first sight. His military experience before he joined Liu Bocheng in the Taihang region had been somewhat limited and not particularly successful. The Bose and Longzhou Uprisings in 1929 and 1930 initially met with almost no resistance, and when they did – from the Nationalists and the French – Deng and his forces retreated. The 7th Red Army was eventually forced to retreat well across country to Jiangxi, with its two commanders being separated on the way and its numbers extremely depleted. On the Long March, Deng's role appears to have been totally political.

Given his background it would be reasonable to assume that his appointment as Political Commissar of the 129th Division at the beginning of 1938 was political and indeed it was. The 129th Division was formed from troops who had been commanded by one of Mao's challengers for the leadership of the CCP on the Long March. When Deng was appointed it was presumably at the behest of Mao Zedong and the leadership in Yan'an who wanted to ensure a measure of control.

However, during the Sino–Japanese War Deng's political and organizational abilities became military skills and he rapidly developed a reputation, which has lasted to this day within the PLA, for being a good soldier and leader. In 1937 when the 129th Division, at that time without Deng, had entered the Taihang region it had about 6,000 men; by 1940 the 129th Division had grown to 200,000. Deng's first real military achievement was the creation of a substantial armed force, which later went on to become the 2nd Field Army, from a very unpromising resource base.

A Preliminary Assessment

Considerable emphasis is usually placed on the extent to which the communist forces during the Sino-Japanese War mobilized the peasantry behind appeals to either social reform, nationalism or both. These undoubtedly formed part of Deng's strategy. However, his new recruits were for the most part not tenant farmers (tenancy was in any case very low in the Taihang region) or even landowning peasants, but rather landless labourers and displaced persons (from both the urban and rural workforce) from other parts of China. Deng, with his reputation for being tough, just and strong, offered them comradeship and a measure of security their lives otherwise lacked.

In the 1940s the forces under Liu Bocheng and Deng Xiaoping – first the 129th Division and then the 2nd Field Army – gained a reputation within the CCP that was very different to that of the other communist armies. They were considered the weakest of the communist troops in a number of respects: they were physically weak, had almost no equipment and were the smallest in number. However, Liu and Deng's army was always the most united largely because of the relationship between the two, and this and its solidarity were its strengths.

Deng's role in creating the army he and Liu led rapidly gave him an equal leadership status in the field. Together they led the march south to the Dabie Mountains in 1947 on foot. It was a manoeuvre which by all accounts should not have worked. They did not secure their positions as they went and relied almost totally on the element of surprise for their progress. However, it did open up the central plains of China as a battleground for the ensuing civil war. In that civil war Deng's leadership of the Huai-Hai campaign has obviously been emphasized during the 1980s. Nonetheless, it was real enough. The front committee directing the campaign was given autonomy to act by the CCP, on the understanding that all commands had to go through and be approved by Deng.

Indeed, Mao issued an order to that effect.

Deng's role as a soldier during 1938 to 1949 became very important to his career after 1949. Of course, the majority of party cadres in the years before 1949 were part of the military offensive. However, Deng's involvement with the military had been and was to remain more than normal. He developed a substantial base of support within the PLA which was to come to his aid on more than one occasion when he was in political trouble. This was partly because he impressed military leaders with his actions during 1938 to 1949. It was also because he ensured that he placed so many of his former subordinates from either the 129th Division, the Taihang region, or the 2nd Field Army in positions of importance within the PLA. Indeed, Deng's continued relationship with his former subordinates from Taihang and the 2nd Field Army was by no means confined to military affairs, and came to play an equally significant role in civilian politics.

The politician

Deng's portrayal as a statesman on the international stage is justified even if exaggerated. Throughout the 1970s and 1980s he has done more than any other Chinese leader to promote relations between China and the rest of the world, particularly through the 'open-door policy'. He has visited the USA, Japan, France, East and Southeast Asia, and received visitors in Beijing from all over the world. Particularly during the early 1980s he made skilful use of the international media in furthering China's ends. By world standards his international role has been modest, but by Chinese standards – and China still does in many ways regard itself as the centre of the world, the Middle Kingdom – he has played a considerable international role. Mao Zedong's foreign experience,

A Preliminary Assessment

it should be remembered, was limited to two trips to Moscow.

In domestic politics, Deng has been promoted as the guardian of the CCP and the epitome of its values during the 1980s.[5] Of course, that is precisely the role that all 'pre-eminent', 'supreme', or 'paramount' leaders are required to play, and that was certainly how Mao saw himself, especially during the Cultural Revolution. However, there is considerable ambiguity in that role, and the relationship between party and leader is almost certain to be unstable, as it was in Mao's case. Deng's interpretation of the CCP's values, structures and mission was clearly different to Mao's. Nonetheless, in the final analysis Deng allowed himself, if to a lesser degree, to fall into the same trap of personalizing the CCP for which he had criticized Mao. During the late 1980s Deng's support, or its withdrawal, appears to have determined the fate of both Hu Yaobang and Zhao Ziyang. Certainly it seems that Deng's attitude to the demonstrations of 1989 was a crucial factor in their suppression.

Deng's interpretation of the CCP's role in Chinese society was not newly constructed during the 1980s and appears remarkably consistent from the early 1940s on. He placed a considerably greater emphasis than Mao on the importance of organization and bureaucracy, as well as on the drive for economic modernization. Indeed, where Mao saw mass mobilization as the engine of change, Deng had a more technocratic vision of China's future.

Deng believed that the principle of the party's monopoly of power was inviolate, hence his opposition to the Cultural Revolution, not simply because it involved an attack on the CCP but also because it undermined the CCP's authority. As he said to a meeting of the Young Communist League in July 1958, 'The key issue is that there is only one party. If you hold firm on this point, then whatever mistakes you may make you will remain basically correct.'[6]

Deng Xiaoping

For Deng the CCP had a duty to lead society, and in order to exercise that leadership function it needed to be a distinct organization. Organizational confusion between party and government would only weaken its ability to lead, as would the CCP not being responsible for its own discipline. In Deng's view the strength of the CCP depended on its solidarity and its good relations with the general population. Both depended upon education within the party and the maintenance of organizational norms. There should be discussion and debate within the party until a decision was taken, but once a decision had been taken then everyone should fall into line behind the collective leadership to enable the party to exercise leadership over the rest of society.

Education within the CCP based on Mao Zedong Thought – not Mao's personal ideas but the distilled wisdom of the CCP's collective leadership from before 1949 – could help ensure the party's feelings of solidarity and unity of purpose. However, Deng argued clearly and consistently that in order to ensure the CCP's leadership of society it was necessary to demonstrate the material advantages. During the Sino–Japanese War this was defence and the maintenance of a productive economy in the areas under CCP control. During and after 1949 it was economic modernization. As he said in 1987, when talking to the premier of Czechoslovakia, but as he might have said at any time during the previous 50 years, 'To build socialism it is necessary to develop the productive forces. Poverty is not socialism.'[7]

Because of his emphasis on material development and the need to develop China's intellectual and organizational infrastructure to that end, Deng has sometimes been portrayed outside the PRC solely as an economic modernizer. That would be a mistake, for as the quotation from 1987 just cited indicates, what Deng sought was socialism. Whatever else that meant it certainly entailed a central role for the CCP. In Deng's cosmology economic

A Preliminary Assessment

modernization was a major concern, but the principle of party rule was an even higher priority. Indeed, as the purge of Zhao Ziyang in 1989 indicates to some extent, even the importance of party discipline and party democracy would be sacrificed if necessary to the principle of party rule.

The obvious contrasts with Mao Zedong's views and work-style raise the question of the precise relationship between Deng and Mao. Many commentators outside the PRC have seen Deng as a loyal Maoist for most of his career before the mid-1970s. This, they argue, explains his relatively sudden return to power after his purge in the Cultural Revolution, as well as his rise to the General Secretaryship of the CCP during the 1950s. However, it is an unsatisfactory explanation, not least because it fails to acknowledge the changing nature of the relationship. It also fails to take account of evidence to the contrary which surfaced in the PRC during the 1980s. For example, Ji Dengkui, shortly before he died in 1987, observed that Deng had been sensible and (unlike him) had not always agreed or sided with Mao Zedong in post-1949 politics.[8]

Here it has been suggested that Deng's support for Mao was by no means certain, and always contingent upon the more important issues (for Deng) of party unity and party discipline. Thus he acted against Gao Gang in 1953, was prepared to accept a rectification campaign he was unhappy about in 1957, and did not support Peng Dehuai at the time of the Lushan plenum in 1959, out of more complex reasons than simple loyalty to Mao. On the other hand, this is not to say that Mao did not regard Deng as a loyal supporter.

On the contrary, there is much to be said for the view that Mao believed Deng to be personally loyal. The political relationship between the two dated back to the attacks on the 'Luo Ming line' in 1933 when Deng had essentially been a substitute for Mao in an intra-party conflict. Thereafter Mao appears uncharacteristically to have trusted Deng to an extent which he withheld from others. Deng was sent to the Taihang region in 1938 at least partially in order to keep an eye on the 129th Division for the Yan'an leadership of the CCP. Alone of all the CCP's leaders in the field he was not required to return to Yan'an for the party's major rectification campaign in 1942–3 which finally removed CPSU influence and ensured Mao's control. Deng became General Secretary of the CCP with Mao's support and despite increasing differences on policy there was little evidence of friction between the two until late in 1966. Even during the Cultural Revolution, Deng was not criticized openly by name in the official media.

Deng's relationships with Mao Zedong and Zhou Enlai, and indeed the extent to which he developed a vast network of associates within the CCP, are clearly important aspects of his political biography. However, by far the most important single explanation of Deng's politics lies in the Taihang experience of the Sino–Japanese War. Deng's vision of the politics of change was derived largely from that experience, and the people he met and worked closely with at that time were to form an important network of power and influence. When the history of the Taihang Base Area of the late 1930s and early 1940s was written during the 1980s for publication in an extremely limited edition, Deng Xiaoping's calligraphy was used for the title, in typically Chinese fashion acknowledging the importance of the relationship.

Of course, Deng's Taihang experience gained much of its impetus from the deliberately created 'model' border region centred on Yan'an. It would also be reading too much into the temporary and wartime conditions of the early 1940s to suggest that all Deng's detailed post-1949 policies had their origins there. Nonetheless, the situation in Taihang posed different problems to those encountered in Yan'an, and sometimes required different solutions. Taihang was bigger, more varied and more influenced by

A Preliminary Assessment

the conduct of war. It was also economically more developed. It was surely no accident that the first three PRC Ministers of Finance had all been involved in financial affairs in this one border region during the early 1940s.[9] Deng's concerns with economic construction and production, democratic centralism and the rights of the minority within the CCP, the separation of party and government, and the widest possible popular support mobilized through a variety of techniques were formulated in response to conditions during the Sino–Japanese War.

Certainly, there can be little doubt about the impact of Taihang on Deng's relations with others within the CCP leadership. The results of his efforts in developing the 129th Division have already been discussed. In terms of his relationships with military leaders, it is also probably significant that the headquarters of the entire 8th Route Army were located in the Taihang Base Area, close by Deng, for most of the Sino–Japanese War. This brought him into close contact with those who were to lead the PLA for at least the first 17 years of the PRC, until the Cultural Revolution.

Military affairs apart, the extent to which Deng's former subordinates and associates from the border region centred on Taihang came to occupy positions of importance not only within the CCP Political Bureau but throughout the party is quite remarkable. Particularly after 1966 they provided Deng with a network of support within the CCP's leadership that was second to none. During June 1989 in the aftermath of military intervention in Tiananmen Square much was made in the Western media of the military relationship between the PLA's 27th Army, commonly held to have led the suppression in Beijing, its former Political Commissar Yang Baibing, and his brother Yang Shangkun, the President of the PRC. Equally important was the political relationship which went back 50 years between Deng and Yang Baibing.

Deng Xiaoping

The reformer

Finally, Deng has also been portrayed as the CCP leader most responsible for the introduction of reform. Here too the image is justified though with reservations. Certainly Deng led the assault on the policies and institutions of the Cultural Revolution during the mid-1970s. Certainly too his treatment in 1976 when he was once again purged from the CCP leadership ensured that he became an extremely popular figurehead to lead the drive for economic modernization and the rejection of the Cultural Revolution.

However, the policies which were implemented in and after 1978 were the product of a collective leadership who had worked together for some time within the CCP before the Cultural Revolution. Their ideas on China's development had first been raised in the mid-1950s, notably as articulated at the 8th CCP Congress by Chen Yun. They had been resurrected in the early 1960s as part of the attempted reformulation of economic policy which followed the catastrophe of the Great Leap Forward. In the late 1970s and after the Cultural Revolution those who had been involved in that process almost twenty years earlier were brought together again by Deng Xiaoping, and the 3rd Plenum of the 11th Central Committee in December 1978 was as much their collective victory as Deng's alone.

The historical origins of the policies and practices of the reform era provide the essential clue to Deng's role as a reformer. On the whole he was not an innovator. Unlike a Gorbachev, he did not proceed from a radical critique of his country's problems to detail a new blueprint. On the contrary, the essence of the reforms launched at the 3rd Plenum was a return to the traditions of the CCP as they had been defined during the early 1950s. The political reforms Deng was responsible for introducing had been foreshadowed in his speech to the

A Preliminary Assessment

8th CCP Congress in 1956, which in turn had drawn heavily on an interpretation of the party's experiences during the 1940s. Deng's emphasis had been on the maintenance of party democracy and on making the political system as efficient as possible, in order to assist economic modernization.

For the most part Deng's innovations during the 1980s were confined to the field of foreign policy. Given the initiative of the 'open door' which followed years of (largely self-imposed) isolation it might seem that this signalled a rather more radical change with the past. However, even here the differences are not as great as may seem at first sight for an approximation of the same policy had been suggested by Chen Yun in and around 1956. On the other hand, one very definitely innovative foreign policy initiative was that which saw Gorbachev visit Beijing in May 1989. It had not been so long since Deng himself had suggested that such a development was impossible.

Deng is essentially a conservative reformer, a traditionalist who wanted to restore what he considered had been the CCP's traditions, which had been set aside during the Cultural Revolution. As he stressed in January 1980 (in a speech to party cadres) support for the CCP had to be renewed through economic growth and a return to the 'conventional ways of doing things.' His definition of Mao Zedong Thought – in terms of three principles: 'seek truth from facts', the mass line and the independence of the Chinese revolution – was that which he had championed during the early 1940s. He repeatedly looked back to that era and resurrected its issues and rhetoric in a contemporary context. Thus, for example, in his speech to the CCP Central Committee shortly after his reinstatement in 1977 he argued for a broad social coalition for change, much as the CCP had established through a policy of promoting a United Front against the Japanese during the late 1930s and early 1940s, when he said, 'One of our party's true great revolutionary weapons, the united front, serves a more useful function than all the weapons used on the battlefield.'[10]

The extent to which Deng sought legitimacy for his reforms in the CCP's traditions may be judged by his adjustment to the history of the 8th CCP Congress of 1956. During the 1980s the 8th CCP Congress was presented as a model congress and its documents were republished in both hard and soft covers. Deng and others pointed to the Congress as having upheld the CCP's traditions and in particular Mao Zedong Thought. Of course, such an interpretation was not completely inconsistent with Mao Zedong Thought as defined by Deng during the 1980s. Paradoxically, though, it had been Deng who had initiated the deletion of reference to Mao Zedong Thought from the CCP Constitution at the 8th CCP Congress.

Deng's need to create tradition in that way highlights the major contradiction in his vision of social and political change. His traditionalism led him to concentrate on the identification of a golden age in the CCP's past – sometimes 1956, sometimes the early 1940s – in order to legitimize contemporary politics. However, that golden age had not necessarily ever existed, or if it had only under certain highly specific and inevitably temporary conditions such as pertained in the revolutionary base areas during the Sino–Japanese War. A vision determined to such an extent by history or tradition is inherently less flexible when faced by radically different circumstances and the new social and political demands generated by economic growth during the 1980s required accommodation rather than Deng's formulaic response.

Deng's legacy to China is ambiguous. He has not only held out the promise of a modernized, industrialized country but has to some considerable extent delivered on that promise. He has created a revolution of rising expectations, which it is unlikely can be confined to

A Preliminary Assessment

economic demands. However, he has clearly not been prepared to meet demands for independent political expression, however low-key those may be. Paradoxically, given Deng's emphasis on the importance of the CCP, the events of June 1989 may not only have made any accommodation between CCP and the urban workforce more difficult to achieve in the short to medium term, they have probably in the long run mortgaged the CCP's future.

References

Introduction

1. CCP Central Committee Department for Research on Party Literature and New China News Agency *Deng Xiaoping* Central Party Literature Publishing House, Beijing 1988. The biography has been extracted from this volume and published separately as *Deng Xiaoping chuanlue* by Renmin chubanshe, Beijing 1988. In the Chinese-speaking world outside China a number of biographies of Deng have been published during the 1980s. Most are based heavily on undocumented rumour and many do not take the new sources of information that have appeared during the 1980s, and subsequent research, into account. Of those probably the best, and certainly the fullest is Han Shanbi *Deng Xiaoping pingzhuan* 3 Vols East West and Culture Publishers, Hong Kong 1988. The late 1980s have seen the publication in English of three biographies of Deng: David Bonavia *Deng* Longman, Hong Kong 1989; Chung Hua Lee *Deng Xiaoping: The Marxist Road to the Forbidden City* Kingston Press, Princeton 1985; and Uli Franz *Deng*

References

   Xiaoping, Harcourt, Brace, Jovanovich, New York, 1989. *Inside China*, an interesting but not necessarily reliable biography of Deng during the Cultural Revolution was published in 1989: Lin Qingshan *Feng yun Shinian, Yu Deng Xiaoping*, PLA Publishing House, Beijing, 1989. The personal recollections of some of Deng's subordinates from 1937–1965 have recently been published in Yang Guoning et al. (ed) *Ershibanianjian – Cong Shizhengwei dao zongshuji*, Shanghai wenyi chubanshe, Shanghai, 1989.
2. Bonavia *Deng* p. 7. Moreover, Deng's uncle Deng Shaosheng went to France at the same time.
3. The account of Deng's life published by the Department for Research on Party Literature of the CCP Central Committee in 1988 records that Deng sailed to France on the *André Lebon*. However, records held in France state that he arrived on the *Porthos*. See Nora Wang 'Deng Xiaoping: The years in France' in *The China Quarterly No 92*.
4. R. Bedeski 'The policial vision of Deng Xiaoping' in *Asian Thought and Society* Vol 13 No 37 January 1988 p. 13.

Chapter 1

1. A recent reviewer of Uli Franz's biography of Deng Xiaoping, queried the source of information on Deng's attitude to croissants and his purchase of several in Paris en route to Beijing in 1974. The source is Yang Shangkun, and the story appears in Harrison Salisbury *The Long March: the untold story* Harper & Row, New York 1985, p. 137.
2. N. Wang 'Deng Xiaoping: The years in France' in *The China Quarterly* No 92.
3. Franz *Deng Xiaoping* p. 47.
4. Edgar Snow *Red Star over China* Gollancz, London 1968, p. 499.

Deng Xiaoping

5. Sources on events in Bose at this time include: 'The Bose Uprising' *Beijing Review* No 6, 1979, 9 February 1979; and Diana Lary *Region and Nation: The Kwangsi Clique in Chinese Politics 1925-1937* Cambridge University Press, London 1974, p. 102-8 'The Chuang peasant movement and soviet.'
6. There are no detailed accounts in English of the Taihang Revolutionary Base Area, or the Shanxi-Hebei-Shandong-Henan Border Region. Sources in Chinese include: Shanxi Provincial Committee of the CCP, Historical Research Section *Wenxian xuanbian* 7 Vols, Shanxi Renmin chubanshe, Taiyuan 1986; Committee to Edit the History of the Taihang Revolutionary Base Area *Taihang geming genjudi shigao* Shanxi Renmin chubanshe, Taiyuan 1987; Qi Wu (ed) *Yige geming genjudi de chengzhang: Kangri zhanzheng he jiefang zhanzheng shiqi de Jin Qi Lu Yu bianqu gaikuang*, Renmin chubanshe, Beijing 1958; and Editorial Group for the compilation of the History of the Taiyue Revolutionary Base Area, *Taiyue gening genjudi jishi* Shanxi Renmin chubanshe, Taiyuan, 1989.
7. The policy became general throughout the CCP areas of control after the beginning of 1942, and was modelled on the experience of Wang Zhen's brigade based at Nanniwan in the Shaanxi-Gansu-Ningxia Border Region. For all of 1937-9, Wang Zhen and his brigade had operated in the area to the south-west of Beijing bounded by the Beijing-Wuhan railway and the Taihang Mountains, before being posted to Yan'an.
8. Deng Xiaoping 'Taihang qu de jingji jianshe' in *Deng Xiaoping wenxuan (1938-1965)* Renmin chubanshe, Beijing 1989, p. 86. The earlier and slightly different version of this speech in English may be found as 'Economic reconstruction in the Tai-hang region' in S. Gelder *The Chinese Communists* Gollancz, London 1946, p. 200.

References

9. The 17 members of the CCP Political Bureau between 1949 and 1989, who had served in the border region centred on the Taihang Revolutionary Base Area during 1938–47 were: Deng Xiaoping, Bo Yibo, Liu Bocheng, Xie Fuzhi, Song Renqiong, Xu Xiangqian, Chen Xilian, Ji Dengkui, Li Desheng, Li Xuefeng, Xu Shiyou, Su Zhenhua, Zhao Ziyang, Qin Jiwei, Yang Dezhi, Wan Li, and Tian Jiyun.

Chapter 2

1. Deng Xiaoping 'Work report to the Southwest Military and Administrative Committee for 1950' in *Zhengfu Gongzuo Baogao Huibian 1950* Renmin chubanshe, Beijing 1951, p. 991.
2. F.C. Teiwes 'Establishment and consolidation of the new regime' in R MacFarquhar and J.K. Fairbank *The Cambridge History of China Vol 14 The People's Republic, Part I: The Emergence of Revolutionary China 1949–1965* Cambridge University Press, London 1987, p. 97.
3. Khrushchev *Khrushchev Remembers* 2 vols Penguin, London 1977: Vol 2, p. 301.
4. Deng Xiaoping *Deng Xiaoping wenxuan (1938–1965)* p. 8.
5. Bonavia *Deng* p. 76; D.W. Chang *Zhou Enlai and Deng Xiaoping in The Chinese Leadership Succession Crisis* University Press of America, London 1984, p. 126.
6. Deng Xiaoping [Teng Hsiao-ping] 'Report on the Revision of the Constitution of the Communist Party of China' in *Eighth National Congress of the Communist Party of China Vol I* Documents Foreign Languages Press, Peking 1956, p. 200.
7. Deng Xiaoping 'Marxism–Leninism Needs to be Integrated with China's Reality' (November 1956) in *Beijing Review* 18 September 1989, p. 14.

8. Deng Xiaoping 'The Communist Party Must Accept Supervision' (April 1957) in *Beijing Review* 25 September 1989, p. 16.
9. Deng Xiaoping 'Guanyu chengfeng yundong de baogao' in CCP Party School Research Section on Party History *Zhonggong dangshi cankao ziliao Vol 8* Renmin chubanshe, Beijing 1980, p. 635.
10. 'Comrade Deng Xiaoping in Zunyi' in *Guizhou ribao* (The Guizhou Daily) 13 November 1958, p. 1. The newspaper story actually comments that when Deng made his suggestion the local CCP secretary 'could only smile, as he himself had not been able to make such a thorough analysis of the situation.'
11. MacFarquhar's interpretation of Deng's absence is in R. MacFarquhar *Origins of the Cultural Revolution Vol I & II*, Oxford University Press, London 1974 & 1983: Vol 2 p. 229, and footnote 209 on p. 407.

Chapter 3

1. See, for example: Deng Xiaoping 'The present situation and the tasks before us' in *Selected Works of Deng Xiaoping (1975-1982)* Foreign Languages Press, Beijing 1984, p. 253; and 'Fayang dang de xiuliang chuantong he zuofeng' in CCP Party School Party Construction and Education Section *Dangfeng wenti* Zhonggong zhongyang dangxiao chubanshe, Beijing 1981, p. 2.
2. Deng Xiaoping 'Zenyang huifu nongye shengchan' in *Deng Xiaoping Wenxuan* (1938-1965) p. 305.
3. Qiu Zhizhuo 'Deng Xiaoping zai 1969-1972' in *Huaren shijie No 1* 1988, p. 142.
4. Other examples of Deng's antipathy are recorded in D. Wilson *Mao, The People's Emperor* Hutchinson, London 1979, p. 379.
5. M Schoenhals 'Unofficial and official histories of the

Cultural Revolution – a review article' in *Journal of Asian Studies Vol 48* No 3 (1989) p. 564.
6. Cultural Revolution sources, which include detail on Deng's activities during the early 1960s as well as during the Cultural Revolution itself, include: Investigation team of Tianjin University August 13 Red Guards Liaison Station for Criticizing Liu, Deng and Tao *Bayisan hongweibing* 17 April 1967; The Capital Liaison Committee to Totally Smash the counter-revolutionary Revisionist Line of Liu and Deng *Chedi cuihui Liu Deng fangeming xiuzhengzhuyi luxian* Beijing, 12 April 1967; Beijing Institute of Physical Education for Workers, Peasants and Soldiers *Dadao Deng Xiaoping* Beijing, March 1967; First division of the People's University Three-Red Grab Liu and Deng Group of the Capital Red Guard Congress *Deng Xiaoping fandang fanshehuizhuyi fanMao Zedong sixiang di yanlun zhaibian* Beijing, April 1967; The East is Red Commune of the Central Committee of the CCP's United Front Work Department *Deng Xiaoping zai tongyi zhanxian, minzu, zongjiao gongzuo ganfmian di fangeming xiuzhengzhuyi yanlun huibian* Beijing, July 1967; The Red Flag Commune of Beijing Railways Institute *He qi du ye!* Beijing, April 1967, translated in *Survey of the China Mainland Press* (Supplement) No 208 p. 1; *and Deng Xiaoping zibaishu* reprinted from several Red Guard Sources in *Zhonggong yanjiu* November 1969, p. 90, and translated in *Chinese Law and Government Vol 3 No 4*, p. 278.
7. Capital Forestry Revolutionaries *Yuanlin geming No 4* Beijing Forestry Institute, Beijing 1967, p. 4.

Chapter 4

1. Information on Deng's life at this time is taken largely

Deng Xiaoping

from three sources. His daughter Deng Rong [Maomao] has written 'Zai Jiangxi de rizili' in *Renmin ribao* 22 August 1984 p. 3: translated as 'My father's days in Jiangxi' in *Beijing Review* No 36 1984, 3 September 1984. This account also appears in Zhou Ming (ed) *Lishi zai zheli chensi* Vol 1 Huaxia chubanshe, Beijing 1986, p. 91. The second source of information is Qiu Zhizhuo 'Deng Xiaoping zai 1969–1972' in *Huaren shijie No 1* 1988. The third is Lin Qingshan *Fengyun shinian yu Deng Xiaoping*, PLA Publishing House, Beijing, 1989.
2. Versions of these documents are contained in Chi Hsin *The Case of the Gang of Four* Cosmos, Hong Kong 1977.
3. Deng Xiaoping *Selected Works of Deng Xiaoping*, in particular 'The task of consolidating the army' p. 27.
4. Deng Xiaoping *Selected Works of Deng Xiaoping*, p. 49.
5. *South China Morning Post* 26 March 1988, Saturday Review p. 1.
6. Deng's closing speech to the congress was published in the daily report from the *New China News Agency* 18 August 1977.

Chapter 5

1. Deng Xiaoping 'Emancipate the mind, seek truth from facts and unite as one in looking to the future' in *Selected Works of Deng Xiaoping*, in particular p. 159.
2. Deng Xiaoping 'Uphold the four cardinal principles' in *Selected Works of Deng Xiaoping*, p. 166.
3. *Selected Works of Deng Xiaoping* p. 302.
4. See, for example: Deng Xiaoping 'Senior cadres should take the lead in maintaining and enriching the party's fine traditions' (2 November 1979) in *Selected Works of Deng Xiaoping* p. 208.

References

5. Deng Xiaoping 'We shall speed up reform' (12 June 1987) in *Fundamental Issues in Present-Day China* Foreign Languages Press, Beijing 1987, p. 192.
6. Deng Xiaoping 'We shall draw on historical experience and guard against erroneous tendencies' in *Fundamental Issues in Present-Day China* p. 184.
7. Deng Xiaoping 'Fazhan zhong mei guanxi de yuanze liyang' (4 January 1981) in CCP Central Committee Document Research Section *San zhong quanhui yilai: zhongyao wenxian xuanbian* Renmin chubanshe, Beijing 1982, Vol 2 p. 649.
8. Deng Xiaoping [Teng Hsiao-p'ing] 'Talk at the Third Plenary Session of the Tenth CCPCC' (20 July 1977) in *Issues & Studies*, July 1978, p. 103.
9. You Ji and Ian Wilson 'Leadership politics in the Chinese party-army state: The fall of Zhao Ziyang' Working Paper 195, The Strategic and Defence Studies Centre, Australian National University, 1989: in particular Table 3, which lists the senior military figures and their backgrounds.
10. L. Dittmer 'China in 1988: the continuing dilemma of socialist reform' in *Asian Survey Vol 29* No 1 (1989) p. 20.
11. Deng Xiaoping 'Talks with Li Peng and Yang Shangkun, 25 April 1989' in *South China Morning Post* 31 May 1989, p. 12.
12. Deng Xiaoping 'Speech at Martial Law Headquarters, 9 June 1989' in *South China Morning Post* 20 June 1989, p. 8; and 'Zai jiejian shoudu jieyan budui jun yishang ganbu shi de jianghua' in 28 June 1989 *Renmin ribao*.
13. *Deng Xiaoping yi si* The Patriotic Publishing Company, Hong Kong 1989, p. 17.
14. 'Deng meets last guests in official capacity' in *China Daily*, 14 November 1989, p. 1.

Chapter 6

1. Deng Rong 'My father's days in Jiangxi' p. 18.
2. Tanjug (Yugoslav News Agency) 23 July 1977, translated in *BBC Summary of World Broadcasts FE/5574*.
3. E. Rice *Mao's Way* University of California Press, Berkeley 1972, p. 262.
4. For example: Suo Yunping, Wang Chaozhu, Liu Xing 'The decisive Huai Hai campaign' in *Jiefangjun wenyi No 5*, 1988, p. 78.
5. Deng's speeches and writings, and commentaries on them have been published in large number during the 1980s. In addition to the volumes already cited in these notes, those include *Deng Xiaoping tongzhi zhongyao tanhua* (February to July 1987) Renmin chubanshe, Beijing 1987; Jiangxi Academy of Social Sciences *Deng Xiaoping de sixiang chutan* Jiangxi renmin chubanshe 1988; Pan Songting, Huang Hai et al '*Deng Xiaoping wenxuan*' *xuexi tiyao* Jiangsu renmin chubanshe 1983; Wu Jiaxiang *Deng Xiaoping: Sixiang yu shijian (1977-1987)* Hunan Renmin Chubanshe, Changsha 1988; and Zang Leyuan, Wang Yongshan, Mu Xiukun (eds) *Deng Xiaoping sixiang yanjiu* Guangxi renmin chubanshe 1988.
6. First division of the People's University Three-Red Grab Liu and Deng Group of the Capital Red Guard Congress *Deng Xiaoping fandang fanshehuizhuyi fanMao Zedong sixiang di yanlun zhaibian* Beijing, April 1967.
7. Deng Xiaoping 'We must continue to build socialism and eliminate poverty' in *Fundamental Issues in Present-Day China* p. 178.
8. Ji Dengkui 'wo shi zhongguo lishishang de yi wei beiju renwu ...' in *Zhongguo dabeiju renwu*, People's University Publishing House, Beijing, 1989, p. 3.
9. The three were Bo Yibo, Rong Zihe, and Deng Xiaoping.
10. Deng Xiaoping 'Talk at the Third Plenary Session of the Tenth CCPCC' p. 105.

Select Bibliography

This section provides a brief guide to further reading on some of the topics raised in this volume. It makes no claim to be comprehensive, and only refers to books available in English.

There are two full-length biographies of Deng Xiaoping already published. One is *Deng Xiaoping: China's reformer* by Uli Franz (Harcourt Brace Jovanovich, New York, 1989). It is a lively and detailed read which concentrates largely on the earlier part of Deng's career. The other is *Deng Xiaoping* by David Bonavia (Longman, Hong Kong, 1989). Because its author unfortunately died in the middle of its preparation, the text remains somewhat episodic and difficult to read. It is, however, a mine of information.

Two good and relatively up-to-date introductions to China's politics and society are B. Womack and J. Townsend *Politics in China* (Little, Brown, Boston, 1986) and M. Blecher *China: Politics, Economy and Society* (Frances Pinter, London, 1986). An informed and straightforward history of the PRC since 1949 is C. Dietrich's *People's China* (Oxford University Press, New York, 1986). However, these three books were designed essentially as student texts. A less formal, but eminently readable introduction to the history and politics of the CCP is Harrison Salisbury's *The Long March* (Macmillan, London, 1985). The story of the Long March is of course a gripping epic. Nonetheless, Salisbury's sources and style make this an excellent read for all audiences.

Zhang Xinxin and Sang *Ye Chinese Lives* (Macmillan, London, 1987) and Paul Theroux *Riding the Iron Rooster* (Penguin, London, 1989) both provide a lively read and an interesting introduction to Chinese society. *Ye Chinese Lives* is an oral history executed by two Chinese journalists. In the book individuals in China's rapidly changing society of the 1980s record their own observations of those changes and their reactions. Paul Theroux spent over a year travelling around China by train, meeting and talking to people. His observations in *Riding the Iron Rooster* are acute and China is well, though often not flatteringly described.

Chinese literature can often supply considerable information about life in the PRC. This has been particularly true for the reform era, when literature has been able to break out of the straight-jacket imposed on it for the decade of the Cultural Revolution. Most of this literature is short stories, and much has been published in English. There are a number of collections of recent short stories including P. Link (ed) *Roses and Thorns* (University of California Press, Berkeley, 1984) and *Stubborn Weeds* (Blond & Briggs, London, 1984); J. Tai (ed) *Spring Bamboo* (Random House, New York, 1989); Lee Yee (ed) *The New Realism* (Hippocrene Books, New York, 1983), and Nienling Liu (ed) *The Rose Coloured Dinner* (Joint Publishing, Hong Kong, 1988).

The reform era itself has spawned a large literature attempting to keep pace with change in China. Necessarily, much of this has proved to be outdated almost as soon as published. Ezra Vogel *One step ahead in China* (Harvard University Press, London, 1989) is unlikely to

Select Bibliography

be in that category. It is a case study of Guangdong province, one of the main foci of reform, during the decade 1978–88. B. Benewick and P. Wingrove (ed) *Reforming the Revolution* (Macmillan, London, 1988) provides a series of informative essays on different aspects of the reform process. Finally, D. Goodman and G. Segal (ed) *China at Forty: Mid-Life Crisis?* (Oxford University Press, Oxford, 1989), though written before the crisis of the late 1980s came to a head in Tiananmen Square in June 1989, nonetheless addresses its origins.

Index

Anhui province, 71, 114
'Anti-Party Clique', 73
'Anti-Rightist Campaign', 68
Anyuan county, 44
Asia, East and Southeast, 142

Baoan, 16
Bayeux, 32
Beijing, 2-3, 11-12, 17-18, 31, 49, 55, 61, 81, 88, 94-6, 103-5, 108-9, 112, 115, 122, 130-32, 134-5, 137, 142, 147, 149; University, 12; Massacre, 52, 69
Bo Yibo, 52-3, 61, 80, 109, 112, 116, 131
Bose Uprising, 40-43, 140
Bose Uprising, The, 134
Bucharest Conference of the Romanian Workers' Party, 89
Bukharin, Nikolai, 35

Cai, Hesen, 32-4
Cai Yuanpei, 11
Canton, 14-15, 40; Military Region, 105-6
Canton Work Conference (of the CCP), 79
'Capitalist Road', 76-7
CCP, *see* Chinese Communist Party
Central Bureau of Soviet Affairs, 43
Central Plains Field Army, *see under* PLA, 2nd Field Army

Central Work Conference (of the CCP), 81-2, 107, 109, 114
Changguanlou group, 81
Changsha, Hunan province, 32
Chen Boda, 91, 138
Chen Duxiu, 34, 37-8
Chen Shaoyu (Wang Ming), 35
Chen Xilian, 98
Chen Yi, 55, 96, 139
Chen Yonggui, 98
Chen Yun, 19-20, 22, 28, 60, 70, 73, 80, 97, 106, 112-13, 115, 119, 124, 126, 129, 131, 148-9
Chengdu, Sichuan province, 8, 10
Chiang Ching-Kuo, 35-6
Chiang Kai-shek, 13-16, 36-7, 40, 54; Japanese invasion threat, 15-17; Northern Expedition, 36; Fourth Encirclement Campaign, 45
China, 16-17, 34, 36, 50, 56-8, 86, 99-100; politics of, 1-7, 18-29, 42, 102, 106; Communist Party, 3; Civil War, 6-7, 17, 48, 53-4, 59-60, 93, 140; worker students, 11, 31-5; breakdown of central authority, 12; uprisings in, 14, 35-8; purges in, 25; non-Chinese groups, 39; internationally isolated, 76; future of, 77; military and economic aid, 88; economic policy, 100, 112, 113, 114-15, 121-4, 148; capitalism in, 102;

Index

foreign policy, 112; inflationary crisis, 129–30
Chinese Communist Party (CCP), 1–7, 13, 15, 24; visions of reform, 4, 14, 18, 45, 58, 112–32; foundation of, 12; relations with Nationalist Party, 12–14, 35–6, 47, 50, 87; relations with Comintern, 13–14; headquarters in Shanghai, 14, 37; rural guerrilla bases or 'soviets', 14–17, 45, 51; struggles for power, 14, 30, 151; headquarters moved to Ruijin, 15; leadership and party unity, 15, 24–9, 55, 60–61, 70, 124–6; '28 Bolsheviks', 15, 35–6, 43, 45, 47, 61; base at Baoan, 16; base at Yan'an, 16, 51; and the Long March, 16; problems of, 18; collectivization, 20; Political Bureau, 20, 27, 52–3, 60, 98, 112, 105, 107, 117–18, 121, 126–7, 129–31, 147; rectification campaign, 21, 66–9; economic situation, 22, 79; split in, 22, 37–8; leaders of, 26, 76, 94, 102; changes in policy, 26–8; party factionalism, 26–7, 93, 101; loyalty ties, 28; demonstration in Paris, 34; underground activities, 37; expansion, 39; Peasant Movement Training Institute, 39–40; income from opium, 41; programme of organization, 41, 58, 62–5; renewed policy of urban insurrection, 42; headquarters moved to Jiangxi, 43; relations with Mao, 45–7; *Struggle*, party's journal, 46; turning point, 47; work of political commissars, 48–9; Taihang region, major base, 49; and nationalist Army, 54–5; Deng becomes General Secretary, 56, 62; minority nationalities, 58; relations with CPSU, 59, 87–90, 112, 122; Constitution, 62–3, 150; journal *Party Life*, 63; open debates, 64–5; criticism of, 68; nuclear technology, 87–9; relations with PLA, 94, 139–40; 'Gang of Four', 113, 116–17; 'Resolution on CCP history', 116–17; 'Guiding Principles for Inner-Party Life', 119; Central Advisory Commission, 119, 131; Central Discipline and Control Commission, 119; United Front, 149
Chinese Communist Party Central Committee, 20, 37, 46, 48–9, 74, 87, 91, 94, 96, 103, 107, 119, 129, 149; Secretariat, 37, 61, 72, 80, 82, 128; 3rd plenum of the 8th Central Committee, 68; 3rd plenum of the 10th Central Committee, 122; 3rd plenum of the 11th Central Committee, 105–110, 111, 115, 148; 6th plenum of the 11th Central Committee, 116; 6th plenum of the 12th Central Committee, 128; 5th plenum of the 13th Central Committee, 134
Chinese Communist Party Congress, 106; 6th, 38; 8th, 20–21, 56, 60–66, 69–70, 81, 89, 101; 148–50; 9th, 94–5; 10th, 98–9; 11th, 107; 12th, 119–20, 125; 13th, 128
Chinese Revolutionary Party, 11
Chongqing, 8–11, 17, 57, 136
Chongyi, Jiangxi province, 43
Civil War/War of Liberation, 6–7, 17, 48, 53–4, 59–60, 93, 140
Collége de Montargis, 33
Comintern, 12–13, 15, 36–8; relations with CCP, 13–14, 16, 18
Communist League of Yugoslavia, 113
Communist Party of the Soviet Union (CPSU), 13, 22, 35, 48,

Index

CPSU (continued)
59, 64, 71, 74, 87–90, 146; 20th Congress, 63, 66, 86; relations with CCP, 59, 87–90, 112, 122
Counter Cultural Revolution, 108
CPSU, *see* Communist Party of the Soviet Union
Cultural Revolution, 2, 7, 9, 23, 25–6, 28, 31, 63, 68, 74, 76–7, 82, 85–6, 90–91, 93–4, 95–107, 108–9, 111–14, 116–20, 123, 135–6, 138–9, 143, 145–9; Group, 91
Czechoslovakia, 141

Dabie Mountains, 54–5, 139, 141
Dazhai, 98
Deng Ken (brother), 9
Deng Maomao (daughter), 137
Deng Pufang (son), 96
Deng Shuping (brother), 9, 57
Deng Wenming (father), 8–10; marriages and children, 8–9
Deng Xianlie (sister), 9, 57
Deng Xiaoping: capitalist and world's favourite communist, 1; leader of CCP, 1–2, 76; leader of PRC, 1; television appearances, 2, 132; *Time* magazine's Man of the Year 1985, 2; world tour, 2; 'Butcher of Beijing', 2–3; visions of party unity, democracy and discipline, 3, 5–6, 56, 58, 61, 64–5, 68, 101, 110–12, 115–17, 120, 126–7, 135, 144–5, 149; character and appearance, 3, 5, 8, 44, 83–4, 90–91, 130, 136–7, 141; nationalism/socialism, 3, 63, 115, 122, 144; early life, 3, 6, 7; dismissals from office, 3–4, 23, 28, 99, 102–103, 105–6; vision of social development, 4; speeches, 5, 34–5, 62, 64–6, 69, 83–5, 100, 118, 128, 148–9; discourages own biography, 5; central influence in China's politics, 6; formation of one of PLA's armies, 6; in France, 6, 8, 10, 30–35, 142; political career, 6, 11, 28–9, 30, 33–6, 56, 59–60; birth, 7; military engagements, 7; name changes, 7, 14, 37, 39; family man, 8–10, 57, 95–6, 136–7; schooldays, 10; leaves Shanghai for France, 11–12; returns to China, 13, 30, 36; sent to Guangxi province, 14–15, 38, 40, 139; disciplined by CCP, 15, 30; promotions in CCP, 16, 60–61; and Taihang region, 17, 51–2, 62–3, 67, 69, 77, 83, 98, 105, 114, 118, 125, 140–42, 146–7; Civil War/War of Liberation, 17, 139; appointed leading party cadre in south-west, 18; member of CCP Political Bureau and Secretary-General of CCP Central Committee, 20; becomes Vice-Premier of the Government Administrative Council (later the State Council), 20, 59, 98–9; elected General Secretary of CCP, 20, 56, 62, 145; internal exile 1969, 23; restored to office 1973, 24, 97, 98; rise and fall from office, 24–5; age structure of leaders, 26; loyalty ties, 28, 30, 55, 93, 97–8, 108; as 'capitalist roader', 28, 96; relations with Mao, 28, 43–6, 48, 56–7, 63–6, 72, 74–5, 77, 79–80, 91, 96, 102, 144–6; visits to USA, 31, 122, 142; taste for French food, 31; police record in France, 32, 34; political and organizational skills, 33, 39, 48–50, 57–8, 61–5, 80–81, 139–40; relations with Li Weihan, 33, 46; joins CCP, 34; editor of *Red Light*, 34; visits to Moscow, 35–6, 74, 87, 89; appointed chief secretary of the Central Committee, 37, 47, 49; marriages, 38, 44, 48; and 6th CCP Congress, 38; becomes political commissar

Index

of 7th Red Army, 41–3; establishes 8th Red Army, 41; CCP adopts renewed policy of urban insurrection, 42; sent to Jiangxi, 43, 93, 137; appointment as party secretary of Ruijin county, 43–4; transferred to Huichang county, 44; becomes director of the Propaganda Department of the Jiangxi CCP Committee, 45; political disgrace, 45; opposition to CCP leadership, 45; divorce from Jin Weiying, 46; appointed secretary general to General Political Department of 1st Front Army, 46; posted in disgrace to Nancun district CCP committee, 46; assigned to General Political Department of 1st Front Army, 46; loses position, imprisoned and interrogated, 46; health, 46–7, 74, 95; participation in the Long March, 46–7, 140; editor of *Red Star* army journal, 46–7; expedition to Shaanxi, 47; appointed head of Propaganda Division of the Political Department of the First Army Group, 47; appointed Deputy Director, then Director of the Political Department of the First Army Group, 47; appointed Deputy Director of the Political Department of the 8th Route Army, 47; CCP Central Committee meeting, 48; meeting of CCP Political Bureau, 48; visits to Yan'an, 48; appointed Political Commissar to 129th Division of 8th Route Army, 48–9, 51, 139–41, 146–7; economic policy, 51–2, 82–3, 100–102, 114–15, 122, 145; vision of politics of change, 52, 146; Battles of Shangdang and Handan, 54; in Taiyue base area, 53; lecturer at Resist Japan University, 53; Chiang Kai-shek's 'dumbbell strategy', 54; leading secretary of East China Bureau, 54; Huai-Hai Campaign, 54–5, 96, 141; military and political contributions, 55; leading 2nd Field Army, 57, 140–1; and South-west Military and Administrative Committee, 57–9; member of State Planning Commission and the Minister of Finance, 59; rural soviet established in north Shaanxi, 60; National Party Conferences 1955, 60; and Gao Gang, 60; responsibility for CCP Constitution, 62; at 8th CCP Congress, 62, 64–5, 66, 81, 149–50; attends 20th Congress of CPSU in Moscow, 63, 66, 88–9; policy of rectification, 66–9, 82; denounces 'extended democracy', 68, 120; reports to 3rd plenum of the 8th Central Committee, 68–9; arguments for collective leadership, 69–70; writings of, 69, 133; and Great Leap Forward, 71–5, 82; meeting of CCP Secretariat, 72; attends formal plenum of the Central Committee, 73; relations with Peng Zhen, 77, 79–80; reform era, 77, 80–82, 111–32, 148–51; mobilization and the 'mass line', 81; at Central Work Conference, 81; Communist Youth League, 82–3; and Jiang Qing, 86; and Sino-Soviet relations, 86–7; head of Anti-Revisionist Writing Group, 87, 90; attends 40th anniversary celebrations of Russian revolution, 89; negotiations with Khrushchev, 88–9; new Cultural Revolution Group, 91; on Mao's attack on CCP leadership, 90–91;

Index

Deng Xiaoping (continued)
imprisonment, 93; purged leaders, 94, 101–102; news of Lin Biao's death, 96; letter to CCP Central Committee, 96; first post-Cultural Revolution public appearance, 96; opposed to politics of mobilization, 98; relations with 'Gang of Four', 97–9, 109, 116; leads delegation to United Nations 1974, 99; reappointed to CCP Political Bureau and Military Affairs Commission, 99; replaces Zhou Enlai, 99; new policy agenda 'Four Modernizations', 99–100, 103, 108–9; importance of classroom education, 100; trial by allegory, 102; revisionist, 102; and capitalism, 102; foreign affairs/policy, 102–103, 112, 121–2, 149; as successor to Mao and Zhou, 103; attacks on, 103; demonstrations in support of, 103; official media, 105, 132–3; exile in Canton, 106; relations with Hua Guofeng, 106–8; reinstatement to all original positions, 107; secure position of, 108; visits East and South East Asia, 108, 142; mistakes, 109; close associates, 109; conditions for recall, 109; become real leader of CCP, 109–110; retirement, 111, 128, 134; 3rd plenum of the 11th Central Committee, 112, 148; 'open door' policy, 112, 121, 142; leading party secretary in Anhui province, 114; 'Four basic principles' for political behaviour, 115, 120, 132; rejection of Cultural Revolution, 116, 119; against 'bourgeois liberalization', 120, 128; at 12th CCP Congress, 121, 128; and future of Hong Kong, 122; and future of Taiwan, 123; reform of PLA, 124–5; distinguished war record, 125; appointed Chairman of the Central Military Commission, 125; relations with Hu Yaobang, 127–8; student demonstrations, Tiananmen Square, 130–2, 135; film release, 133–4; assessment of, 135–51; tour of provinces, 137; relations with Yang Shangkun, 138; image as soldier, 139–42; as Vice-Chairman of National Defence Council, 139; Chairman of Military Affairs Committee, 139; Sino-Japanese war, 139–41; visits Japan, 142; role as politician and statesman, 142–47; domestic politics, 143; interpretation of CCP's role, 143–4; calligraphy, 146; political relations with Yang Baibing, 147; traditionalism, 150; legacy to China, 149–51; importance of CCP, 151
Donglan, 39–40

Economic policy, 18–20, 21–2, 70–71, 78–9, 80, 100, 111–32, 148; Five Year Plans, 19–20, 70, 123–4, 126

Feng Funeng, 36
Feng Yuxiang, 13, 35–6
France, 3, 6, 8, 10–11, 30–35, 46, 103, 142
French Consulate, 41
Fujian province, 8, 45, 121

'Gang of Four', 98–9, 103–4, 106–7, 109, 113, 116–17
Gansu, 71
Gao Gang, 59–61, 65, 145
Germany, 11
Gorbachev, Mikhail, 2–3, 112, 122, 131–32, 148–9

Index

Great Leap Forward, 22, 26, 53, 56, 65, 69–76, 78, 80–82, 87–88, 92, 148
Guang'an county, 8–10
Guangdon province, 8, 43, 114, 121
Guangxi Clique, 40
Guangxi province, 7, 14–15, 38–41, 43, 45, 139
Guangzhou, Canton province, 42
Guerra, Alfonso, Spanish Vice-Premier, 121
Guilin, Guangxi province, 42
Guizhou province, 9, 57, 71

Hainan Island, 121
Haiphong, Vietnam, 39
Han Chinese, 58
Hebei province, 71
Hebei-Shandong-Henan border area, 49, 53
Hechi, 42
Ho Chi Minh, 31, 39, 90
Hong Kong, 39, 112, 114, 122–3
Hu Qiaomu, 97, 116
Hu Qili, 126
Hu Yaobang, 53, 83, 99, 105, 108, 116–17, 127, 130–31, 137, 143
Hua Guofeng, 24, 103, 105, 107, 109, 113, 115–17, 122, 138
Huai-Hai Campaign, 7, 96, 139
Huai River, 55
Hubei province, 9, 17
Huichang county, 44
Hunan province, 43, 71
'Hundred Flowers Movement', 21, 68–70
Hundred Regiments Campaign, 50
Hungary, 66
Hutchinson's Rubber Factory, Montargis, 33

Japan, 2, 10, 15–17, 121, 142; Liberal Democratic Party, 27
Ji Dengkui, 98, 145
Jiang Qing (Mao's wife), 23–4, 86, 97–9, 103, 138
Jiangsu province, 103

Jiangxi province, 4, 14–15, 42–5, 71, 95–6, 137–8, 140
Jiangxi Soviet, 15–16, 30, 45
Jin Weiying (Deng's second wife), 44, 46, 138
Jinggangshan, 15

Khrushchev, Nikita, 61, 63, 66, 88–9
Kim Il-sung, 133
Korosec, 113, 120

Land reform, 4, 14, 18, 45, 58
Le Creusot Iron and Steel Plant, 32
Le'an county, 46
Left River Valley, 39, 41
Lenin, Vladimir, 3, 12
Li Desheng, 98
Li Lisan, 38, 42–5
Li Mingrui, 38, 40
Li Peng, 126, 130
Li Weihan, 33, 38, 46, 138
Li Xiannian, 80, 106, 112, 131
Li Xuefeng, 98
Li Youying, 11
Li Zongren, 40
Lin Biao, 23–4, 60, 94, 96–8, 101, 117, 138
Liu Bocheng, 7, 30, 48–9, 53–5, 57, 98, 139–41
Liu Lantao, 61–2
Liu Shaoqi, 22–3, 56–7, 59–60, 66, 68, 70, 72, 76–7, 79, 81, 87–9, 94, 117
Liuzhou, Guangxi province, 42
Long March, 36, 43–7, 138, 140
Longzhou Uprising, 41, 140
Lu Dingyi, 80
Luo Ming, 45
'Luo Ming line', 45–6, 61, 138, 145
Lushan Conference (of the CCP), 71–5, 78, 145

MAC, *see* Military and Administrative Committee
Mao Zedong, 1–3, 6, 15–16, 19–20, 25, 27–9, 32–3, 46, 52–3, 56, 59, 76–7, 80, 86, 93–4, 97–8, 103, 107, 108, 116, 120, 128, 135–8,

Index

Mao Zedong (continued)
140, 142–6; Cultural
Revolution, 2, 23–4; character
and personality, 4, 15, 20, 81–2;
'New Democracy', 4; and rural
soviets, 15, 42; establishes
PRC, 18; death, 19, 106–8;
collectivization, 20; Thought,
20, 63–4, 83–91, 101, 108, 111,
113–15, 142, 147–8; and 8th
CCP Congress, 20–21;
economic development, 21–2;
ideas of, 22–3, 26; coup plot
against, 23, 44; inner-party
conflict, 24; age structure of
leaders, 26; relations with
Deng, 30, 43–6, 48, 56–7, 61,
63–6, 74–5, 77, 79–80, 91–2,
94–5, 145–6; struggle for
supremacy, 36; and Long
March, 43–7; relations with
CCP, 45–6, 90–91; attempts to
minimize his influence, 45;
policies adopted, 47; dismissal
of, 65; views on rectification,
67–8, 69–70; at Lushan
Conference, 71–5; skilful
political manipulator, 72–3;
and 'mass line', 81; and
Sino-Soviet relations, 84;
attends 40th anniversary
celebrations of Russian
revolution, 86; and 9th CCP
Congress, 94–5; memorial
meeting for Chen Yi, 96; ill
health, 99, 102; vision of, 83,
100, 102
Mao Zetan (Mao's brother), 138
Manchu (Qing) dynasty, 10
Marseilles, 8, 11, 32–3
Marx, Karl, 3
Marxism–Leninism, 27, 67; Mao
Zedong Thought, 63, 115
May 4th Movement, 11–12
Military and Administrative
Committee (MAC), 18
Minority nationalities, 58
Mongolia, 12, 23, 96
Montargis, France, 32–3, 38

Moscow, 3, 15, 35–6, 38, 43, 46, 63,
74, 87, 89, 143

Nanchang Uprising, 14, 37, 40
Nanjing, 7, 54, 55, 59, 103
Nanning, Guangxi province, 40
National Party Conference (of the
CCP), 60, 111, 126
National People's Congress (NPC),
38, 99, 106, 108
National United Army, 36
Nationalist Party, 6–7, 9, 12–13,
17, 36, 40, 44, 48, 54, 138;
army, 7, 16–17, 41, 43, 50–51,
53–5, 57–9; relations with CCP,
12–14, 35–6, 47, 50; split in, 37;
withdrawal of troops, 50
New China News Agency, 9
New People's Study Society, 32
New York, 31
North Korea, 133
North Shaanxi Soviet, 61
NPC, *see* National People's
Congress
Nyerere, Julius, of Tanzania, 134

Paifang, 8
Paris, 31, 34, 39
Party Life, CCP journal, 63
Peng Dehuai, 22, 60, 65, 71, 72–4,
81, 107, 145
Peng Li, 2
Peng Zhen, 66, 68, 77, 79–80,
89–90, 109, 112, 116–17, 129,
131
People's Communes, 22
People's Daily, 131
People's Liberation Army (PLA),
2, 6–7, 18, 23–5, 57, 72–3, 94,
97, 99–100, 108, 118, 124–6,
132, 135, 140, 147; 1st Field
Army, 57; 2nd Field Army, 48,
53–5, 57, 97, 125, 139–42; 3rd
Field Army, 55, 139; 8th Route
Army, 129th Division, 47–53,
62, 97, 125, 139–42, 146–7;
27th Army, 147; Military
Academy, 59; relations with
CCP, 94, 139–40;

Index

reorganization of, 139
People's Republic of China (PRC), 1–2, 18, 23, 25, 30, 56–7, 76, 94, 100, 112, 120–23, 131, 144–5; allied with Soviet Union, 18; regionalism, 57–60; proposed integration of Hong Kong, 112, 114, 120–21; Ministers of Finance, 147
PLA, *see* People's Liberation Army
Poland, 66
Political reform, 111–32
Porthos Messageries Maritimes liner, 11
PRC, *see* People's Republic of China
Prince Sihanouk, Cambodian leader, 31, 96

Qiao Shi, 126
Qing Ming (Festival of Sweeping the Graves), 103
Qingong jianxue (work-study movement), 11
Qu Qiubai, 38
Quinghua University, 104

Rao Shushi, 59–60, 65
Rectification, 66–9, 82–6
Red Army, 16, 42, 45, 47, 60, 132; 7th, 40–43, 140; 8th, 41–2; *see also* PLA
Red Guards, 23, 63, 76, 91, 94, 96
Red Light, CCP newsletter, 34
Red Star, army journal, 46–7
Reform era, 111–32
Regionalism, 57–60
Renault plant, Billancourt, 31, 33
'Report on the Rectification Campaign', 69
Resist Japan University, 53
'Returned Students Clique', *see* '28 Bolsheviks'
Revolutionary Martyrs Memorial, 103
Right River Soviet, 41–2, 44
Right River Valley, 39–40
Ru river, 54
Ruijin, 15, 43–4

Russia, *see* Soviet Union
Russian Revolution, 48

Shaanxi–Hebei–Henan border, 49
Shaanxi–Hebei–Henan–Shangdong Army, 139; *see also* PLA 2nd Field Army
Shandong, 11, 53
Shanghai, 8, 11, 13–15, 34, 38–9, 42–3, 55
Shanxi province, 17, 47, 53
Sichuan province, 7–9, 11, 32–3, 49, 57, 114
Sihanouk, Prince (Cambodian Leader), 31, 96
Sino-American relations, 87
Sino-Japanese War, 4, 17, 44, 48–51, 53, 93, 95, 97–8, 101, 104–6, 125, 139–41, 144, 146–7, 150
Sino-Soviet relations, 19, 22, 74, 86–9, 94, 122
Snow, Edgar, 16, 33
Socialist Youth League of China, 32–3
Société chinoise d'Education rationelle française, 11
Song Rengiong, 61–2
South-West Military and Administrative Committee, 57
Southern Hebei base area, 50
Soviet Union, 2, 12–13, 18–19, 23, 25, 34–6, 59, 63, 66, 74, 78, 82, 86–90
Special Economic Zones, 114–15, 121
Stalin, Josef, 13–14, 19, 25, 35, 89
State Planning Commission, 99
State Statistical Board, 71
Struggle, CCP party journal, 46
Su Zhenhua, 98
Sun Yat-sen, 12–13; University, 35

Taihang region, 4, 6, 17, 30, 44, 48–52, 62–3, 67, 69, 77, 97–8, 118, 140–42; Revolutionary Base Area, 49, 51, 146–7
Taiyuan, 127
Taiyue base area, 50

Index

Taiwan, 36, 55, 123
Tan Zhenlin, 46, 61–2, 97
Tanzania, 134
Tao Zhu, 109
Tiananmen Square incidents, 2, 18, 103–5, 106, 109, 130–32, 135, 147
Time magazine, 2
Trans-Siberian Railway, 12
Trotsky, Leon, 13, 35
'28 Bolsheviks' ('Returned Students Clique'), 15, 35–6, 43, 45, 47, 61

United Kingdom, 112, 123
United Nations, 2, 99
United States of America, 2, 103, 108–9, 122, 142
University of the Toilers of the East, 35

Versailles Treaty, 11
Vietnam, 109, 122, 124

Wan Li, 105, 112, 114, 128, 137
Wang Dongxing, 96, 105, 122
Wang Hongwen, 98
Wang Jiaxiang, 36, 46, 96
Wang Ming (Chen Shaoyu), 35
Wang Zhen, 96, 106
War of Liberation, *see* Civil War
Water Margin, 102
Wei Baqun, 38, 39–42
Wenhui Bao, Shanghai newspaper, 103
Women's Federation, 38
World War I, 11
World War II, 88
Wu De, 105
Wu Yuzhang, 11
Wuhan, 9, 37

Xia Bogen (Deng's stepmother), 9, 57, 95
Xian, 13, 36; Military Academy, 60
Xie Fuzhi, 98

Xie Jinbi, 57
Xiexing, 8, 10
Xinjian county, 95–6
Xu Shiyou, 98, 105
Xunwu county, 44
Xuzhou, 55

Yan'an, 4, 9, 16–17, 47–8, 51–3, 82, 108, 146
Yang Baibing, 147
Yang Dezhi, 125
Yang Shangkun, 2, 31, 61, 91, 116, 130, 138, 147
Yangtze river, 7–8, 17, 37, 54
Yao Wenyuan, 98, 102
Ye Jianying, 72, 106, 125–6
Young Communist League, 143
Yu Shaojie, 39
Yu Zuobo, 40
Yunnan province, 57

Zhang Chunqiao, 98, 102
Zhang Qianyuan (Deng's first wife), 38
Zhang Wentian, 35–6
Zhang Xiaomei, 38
Zhang Yunyi, 53, 112, 139
Zhao Ziyang, 53, 112, 114, 117, 124, 127–31, 143, 145
Zhou Enlai, 1, 6, 15–16, 22, 24, 29–31, 37–8, 43–4, 59, 70, 72, 77, 88, 93, 95, 97–9, 102–103, 138, 146; establishes Socialist Youth League of China in France, 32; editor of *Red Light*, 34
Zhou Erfu, 119
Zhou Yang, 80
Zhu De, 49, 88
Zhuang (non Chinese group), 39, 42; Peasant Movement, 39–40
Zhuo Lin (Deng's third wife), 48, 95
Zunyi province, 16, 71; Conference, 47